A Girl's Life With God

A Girl's Life With God

Casey Hartley Gibbons

New Hope Publishers
Birmingham, Alabama

New Hope® Publishers
P. O. Box 12065
Birmingham, AL 35202-2065
www.newhopepubl.com

Library of Congress Cataloging-in-Publication Data
Gibbons, Casey Hartley.
A girl's life with God / by Casey Hartley Gibbons.
p. cm.
Summary: Former "Miss American Teen" Casey Hartley Gibbons encourages readers to grow toward maturity in Christ, develop leadership skills, find their unique gifts, learn to minister to others, and recognize that teenagers do not have to wait until adulthood to make a difference in the world.
ISBN 1-56309-757-5 (pbk.)
1. Girls-Religious life. [1. Conduct of life. 2. Christian life. 3. Youths' writings.] I. Title.
BV4551.3.G53 2003
248.8'33—dc21
2003000758

Cover design by Righteous Planet Design, Inc.
Franklin, Tennessee

ISBN: 1-56309-757-5

N034115 • 0503 • 10M1

It is with great honor that I dedicate my first book to my Lord and Savior, Jesus. May He be glorified.

Table of Contents

Acknowledgments

A Girl's Life With God has been an exciting journey. This book is in your hands because of the encouragement of many people. I would like to acknowledge some of those people by giving a brief description of how they have helped me.

The first group I thank is my family. My husband, Scotty Gibbons, is my best friend. He prayed for me when I had a deadline, and he listened to me when I needed to read aloud (and re-read and re-read) chapters. He is the man of my dreams, my one and only. My little girl, Candice, has also been a big supporter. She always stayed quiet and was a perfect angel for me. Well, she wasn't exactly born yet, but as she was growing in my womb I felt as though she was cheering me on! My parents, Rob and Judy Hartley, and my brother, Austin Hartley, have also been a blessing throughout this book project. My dad always encouraged me to hang in there, even when it was my fourth year of writing. My mom was a big help with her amazing ability to pull me through the tragedies of deleted chapters and slow typing. And Austin has always been there to make sure whatever did happen with my writing didn't go to my head. He says that no matter what I write, I'm still just a goober.

The publishing team at New Hope Publishers also deserves to be honored. Rebecca, Lynn, Tamzen, Kristi, and Tara have been great to work with. My prayer is that their ministry in the "book world" would touch more lives than they ever could have imagined. I would like to especially thank Leslie Caldwell of New Hope. She took the time and energy to read my manuscript and believe in its message. She is a sweet friend and I will always be thankful for her heart to see teenage girls excel in the things of God.

I am also thankful for the encouragement of Dr. Joe White. Although he runs the great Christian athletic camp, Kanakuk Kamp, is a well-known speaker, and is an award-winning author, he is outstanding to me because he loves Jesus and he loves teenagers. He supported me and believed in me as a teenager not just with his words, but also with his actions.

Finally, I would like to acknowledge the teenage girls and my friends in Real Life Student Ministries. They have been a support through prayer and love. It is an honor to serve with such an incredible group of God-loving people.

Introduction

If you are a teenage girl who has given her heart to Christ, and you want to be used for His glory during your teen years, this book is for you. This book covers a variety of issues that you may be facing. Attitude, relationships, trials, and self-image are some of the topics discussed. Each chapter begins with a down-to-earth journal entry and ends with a fill-in-the-blank section for you to express your feelings. And everything in between is filled with Scriptures, quizzes, and true stories.

How did this book come about? In the middle of a January night in 1998, I woke up with a pressing urge to write down 10 principles for teenage girls to know. I was eighteen years old and a senior in high school. Less than two months earlier I had won the Miss American Teen title, a division of the American Coed Pageant system ("coed" does not mean that both genders compete. It means well rounded. I know, I wondered too at first). It had been a dream of mine since I started pageants five years earlier.

So there I was. Miss American Teen 1998. I wasn't exactly sure what I would do as a Miss American Teen, but I had some ideas. I figured that if I had one year to hold the title, I should use it to the best of my ability. If I was going to speak to people, I needed to do it with passion and give it my all. However, I didn't feel strongly about any issue as much as I did about God. I felt (and still feel) a passion about His forgiveness, His love, and His gift of life. That's what I wanted to communicate to people. Specifically, I decided that I wanted to communicate it to my own peer group—teenage girls—more than anyone else. Why did I choose my own peers?

Back up one month. So now it is Christmas 1997 (one month after winning). It was in the Galleria Mall in Birmingham, Alabama, that I felt an overwhelming urge to tell other teen girls about Christ. The mall was jam-packed for the holidays. It was lunchtime and I was at the food court. As I sat reserving a table for my family, I noticed the enormous number of teen girls that flooded the mall. (I mean, hello? School was out and the sales were on!) I thought about how I had just won the pageant and how over the next year I would be able to connect with other teens. Teens I normally wouldn't be able to meet. That was a cool thought. But then again, what was I going to say to those girls when I met them? And why would they care about a Miss American Teen?

I came to the conclusion that they probably wouldn't care. That is, unless I communicated a message they wanted to hear. I mean, why should they care? What good is it if Miss American Teen is just a girl, dressed up with a crown and a banner, who smiled and waved at everyone? I had to do more than that. I had to use the title to spread the gospel. That is what would cause girls to listen. It would be the greatest message they could hear.

So there I sat, watching girl after girl go by. All I could think about was telling them about God. I had to think of a way to get to talk to these girls. I wanted to share with them the joy that I was experiencing because of my relationship with Christ. But how could I tell them all? Maybe I could go to all their schools to talk to them. Or maybe I could stay at the mall and stop them at the door. Both options were out. That's when I thought about how other people send their messages out to the world—they write a book. That is what I would do. I would write a book, a book that would reach other teenage girls.

Which brings us back to the January night awakening. So far, all I knew was that I was going to write a book. Being a teen myself, I had no clue exactly what that meant or how to go about it. But what I did know is that in that moment, God was speaking to me about what to write. So I grabbed a pen and a nearby used envelope, and I wrote down ten ways that Christian teen girls could raise the standard during the teenage years. I figured that if I could help develop the Christian girls, they would be able to reach the unsaved girls.

After that initial beginning, a lot happened. Things like losing my suitcase on the way back from a mission trip—the first few chapters were in the suitcase. Who knew not to handwrite a book in your daily journal and take it overseas? That situation was followed by my telling people that I "had a book coming out soon" when I hadn't even sent it to a publisher. Was I lying? Not on purpose. I actually thought that a person writes a book, contacts a publishing company, and then the publishers print it and put it in stores right away. Well, I found out that it doesn't really work that way.

Needless to say, this book has taken time and a lot of learning on my end, but it is finally paying off. It's paying off because you are holding it and reading it. The odds are that you are a teenage girl. Or maybe you are a parent, grandparent, leader, or friend of a teenager. No matter who you are, I am excited that you are interested in seeing teens grow in their walk with Christ.

Since I started the book, I have graduated from high school and college, married a youth pastor, and had a baby. So, I'm not exactly a teen anymore. But I still feel like a teen, and I love teenagers. I love the potential that each teenage girl holds inside of her. I love the influence that a teenage girl has when she devotes herself to God. And I love the testimonies when a teenage girl reaches her family, school, and friends for Christ.

Although I truly believe you will have a blast reading this book, I admit that it may sometimes ask a lot of you. I have written it in a way that will challenge you to evaluate yourself. Sometimes that can be hard to do. I know because I continually have to change and grow in many areas. It is not easy to change. It is especially hard when you may be the only one you know making changes. But don't let that discourage you. Take your time as you move through the pages. You may even want to pause between chapters to see if God is speaking to you about what you just read. Oh, and as you begin, make sure you don't skip Chapter One. It is essential to the heart of the book.

Having said all that, I guess I better let you go so you can begin. I think it is so cool that you are willing to learn more about becoming a godly teenage girl. The fact that you are reading this book says that you have what it takes to do great things for God. And as you apply the principles in this book, *I truly believe that you are about to experience the best days of your teenage life.* See you in Chapter One!

1

Who Are You?

In order to make a difference you must be different.

Dear Journal,

Who am I? There must be more to life than what I see. Everywhere I look, teenagers are making bad decisions. I don't want to be like everyone else. I want to be different. I don't want to just "get through" my teen years. I want to go through them with purpose. I want to make a difference. I want to be my best and help others do the same.

Maybe I'm weird. Maybe I'm not. Who knows? People tell me that all my emotions are extreme because I'm a teenager. I wonder if I'm really an unrealistic dreamer. It's just that I want to do and be something awesome for God. But how?

—Samantha

Have you ever felt like Samantha? Have you ever wanted to be and do something that sets you apart for God's work? Maybe you've seen how poorly other teens, even Christians, are living, and you know there must be a better way. I'm sure you've seen students who claim to follow Christ, but their lifestyles reflect that they are more caught up in the world than *souled out* to God. *Souled out* means completely, totally, wholly giving yourself to God.

It means that your life is 100% in His hands. Your desires, talents, goals, and heart are given over to Him for His glory.

Many teens say they are Christian, but they do the same things people who aren't saved do. Some are involved in premarital sex, alcohol, cigarettes, and drugs. Some girls wear skimpy clothes and are overly flirty. And then other people constantly lie and steal, or always choose to be negative and down. The list could go on forever! The odds are you have been exposed to or even involved in the things that can ruin a girl's life.

But if you, like Samantha, believe there is much more to life than these choices and many other wrong decisions, you are not weird, far out, or an unrealistic dreamer. In fact, *you are a teenager who has the capacity to change the world.* If you feel in your heart that God has given you a desire to be above average in your choices, you are on your way to change the standards of teenagers and lead others around you. Your desire could be small or large, but if you know there is more to being a Christian teenager than attending Sunday school, praying over your sandwich, and going to camp every year, you're on to something.

Miss American Teen

Pause here with me for a second, okay? Before we move on about living above average, let me tell you about myself, so you'll know where I am coming from. I wrote this book because I realized a lot of teenage girls are not living up to their potential in Christ. But don't worry— I'm not some older person trying to run your life. Well, I am older, and I'm married, but at least I'm in my early twenties and it wasn't *too* long ago that I was where you are. In fact, I started getting ideas for this book when I was right in the middle of the teenage world. I was a senior in high school and had just won the Miss American Teen pageant title.

Some of you may be thinking at this point—"Pageants? You've got to be kidding. Already I can't relate to this girl." If that's what you're thinking, it's okay. Not everyone likes or agrees with the idea of pageants. Lots of people think pageants are all about showing off and being a ditz. However, not all pageants are alike; the one I was involved in was family-oriented, judged on overall ability, and it didn't have a swimsuit competition (I was thrilled). In fact, I think it is the greatest pageant system out there for girls because it focuses on the girl as a whole, not just her looks.

Here's how things evolved. It was fall of my senior year, I had competed in the Miss Missouri Teen pageant a couple of months earlier, and now I was headed to the national pageant. The competition was held in Orlando, Florida, at Disney World. More than 4,000 girls had competed on the state levels, and the remaining fifty were in Florida to compete. The week was full and fun. Sunday night was the final night of competition. I was among the top fifteen girls chosen by the judges. Then they began announcing the winners, starting with fourth runner-up. My name wasn't called. That is, not until the last chance, and that's when the emcee said, "Ladies and gentlemen, your new Miss American Teen is . . . Casey Hartley!"

I bet you can picture what happened at this point. Yep. I cried, waved, and starting shaking. Now that I look back, it was hilarious. I remember I didn't even have tears, but I kept wiping my eyes like tears were streaming. It's amazing what you'll do in moments of celebration!

So that is when I began a journey of traveling, speaking, writing, and meeting thousands of other teenage girls. That was also the beginning of the time when God revealed some things to me about others and myself.

When I traveled that year, I had the chance to meet some neat Christian teens. But other times, I would meet Christian teenage girls who were living compromising lifestyles. They claimed to love God, yet they still lived like everyone else. I would ask myself, "Don't they know their life has a purpose and a destiny? Where are their dreams—the dreams that could change the world? They could be incredible, godly teenage girls."

During that time I also evaluated my own heart and made a commitment to change the standards of my own life. I had to take my walk with Christ up a notch so I could make a difference in other girls' lives. I decided to pay attention to details and decisions in my life like never before. I knew I would never be perfect, but I wanted to be a world changer. I did not want to simply exist and be neutral in my walk with Christ. In addition, I didn't want to watch other girls my age fade into the world and never make a difference. That's how this book came about. I wanted to let you know that you can live through your teen years without compromising your walk with God.

What Does That Mean?

It's true. You, through God's grace, can change your life from being *okay* to being *incredible*. You can be different! You can be a pace-setter, starting with your life as it is right now. I know life is full of ups and downs. And every day brings new obstacles, new challenges, and new temptations. Sometimes you will be confronted with issues that you have no control over, while other times you will have the ability to make decisions. And those are the times I am talking about, times when you have the ability to make a choice.

The point is that you can have a different way of living. No matter what comes your way, you can choose to be separate. An example. A person of influence using the talents God has given you. You can have a life that says you are totally committed to God and living for Him. A life of confidence in Christ with a lifestyle that reflects it. What an amazing opportunity!

Say What?

Basically this book is to help you lead an outstanding life as a Christian. It will encourage you not just to proclaim that you believe in Christ and then go on the same as before. It will urge you not to just pray with your head and never follow with your heart. It's about a call to total devotion, a call to 100% commitment. You can take the average standard of your life and raise the mark.

This challenge to 100% devotion is for those who love God but want more of Him. It's for those of you who want to go to extremes for God because He went to extremes for you. God has so many blessings waiting for those who will be totally souled out for Him.

What's the Big Deal?

Why should you want to be this way? Why is it a big deal that you choose to follow the Lord wholeheartedly? Because Scripture teaches us not to be lukewarm. We are to either follow God totally or not at all. If you play on the fence, Scripture is clear about what can happen to you. Revelation 3:15–16 says, "I know your deeds, that you are neither cold nor hot. I wish you were either one or the other! So, because you are lukewarm—neither hot nor cold—I am about to spit you out of my mouth." Whoa! That's major stuff. God must really hate it when we claim to love Him but don't show Him that we do. So you better choose whom you will live for. And what better person than Jesus? Savior of the world. Son of the God of all the universe. The one who died for your sins.

What About the Past?

So what if you want to take this mega-challenge but aren't sure you have what it takes to be different? Guess what? *It's not about where you have been, but where you can go.* It doesn't matter what you have done or how messed up your past is. After you ask God for forgiveness, you can be free. In fact, it says in 1 John 1:9: "If we confess our sins, he is faithful and just and will forgive us our sins and purify us from all unrighteousness." And Jesus said it this way in John 8:36: "So if the Son [Jesus] sets you free, you will be free indeed."

There you go. You ask and God forgives. Don't be held back. There is no need for you to keep thinking about all the wrong you have done. Today is a new day. Just because you haven't been the best up until now does not mean that God can't change you. At this point you can't go back to what has happened, but you can choose what will happen. Your life can start a new path today. Just stop, ask for forgiveness, and change.

Has It Worked for Anyone Else?

Yes, it has worked for others. Take my friend Troy, for example. He did not live for God through high school and college. But God forgave his past and changed him. Troy wanted to get and stay on track and he did. Now he is a leader, and he touches lives every day. Here's his story:

God has really changed my life. I am not what I used to be.

The problems I faced started in junior high. My interests were sports and girls. Popularity was my main priority. It was all I cared about. This priority carried over into high school, except there I tried even harder. If I wasn't playing sports, I was partying. My friends and I seldom did anything without drinking. Alcohol was a major part of my life.

By the time I was in college, I was out of control. All I cared about was having a good time. I kept getting more and more involved in sin. I had been that way for so long that it became who I was. It seemed like no big deal, until someone got hurt.

It was New Year's Eve and my friends and I were partying. We played cards, sang songs, watched TV, and of course, drank. After midnight my friend Matt wanted to go see our buddy Martin across town. So we left, not thinking anything of it. Martin was glad to see us, and we hung out till 2 A.M. and then started to head back to campus. That's when my "fun" world of sin caught up with me.

I was driving, and I sped around a curve too quickly. My car went out of control and we wrecked. I was fine but Matt wasn't. I tried talking to him, but he was unconscious. I went to a nearby house and called 911. When help arrived, I was arrested for drunk driving and taken to jail. After I arrived at jail I found out Matt had died. My bad decisions had cost my friend his life.

The guilt I felt was unbelievable. The next day I was bailed out of jail. All I could do was wait until my court date to see if I would spend seven years in prison. I didn't care what happened to me. I was just scared of facing Matt's family.

I attended the funeral but couldn't imagine what people were thinking about me. That's when I saw God's grace. Matt's family welcomed me with hugs and words of love. I couldn't believe it. Matt's mom said, "You know we forgive you and God will forgive you too if you ask Him. And He can use this tragedy for good."

Three days later I gave my life to God. I understood forgiveness and wanted to give everything to Him. Since then, He has truly blessed me. Some days are hard, but God is with me. On my court date, the judge decided to give me five years probation and then clear my record if all goes right. God has given me many opportunities to share my testimony, and other people have been saved. Now I am in a hard-core discipleship program with opportunities every day to reach out to my community, all because I chose to live a new life.

It's not too late. You can be a new person.

I respect Troy for his decision to start over. Now he is completely different than before, and God has honored him for it. The same can happen for you. You can change today, and God will bless you for your choice. You can move on and make a difference. Don't wait until tragedy happens, like it did in Troy's life.

What is keeping you from being separate from the world's standards? What area in your life is keeping you from being the best for God? Is it that you aren't living for God like you did when you were first saved? Perhaps it is swearing, or music that dishonors God. Maybe you have tried smoking or had sex. Perhaps your friends are pulling you away from God. Only you know what is going on in your heart. You can see these areas that are keeping you from God's ultimate plan for your life.

☞ **Check It Out** _____

Below is a checklist of possible issues you may be facing. These could be stopping you from being totally souled out for the things of God. If you don't change your behavior, these things could destroy your chance of being an example of a godly teenage girl. Check off the ones that you struggle with. Then we will take a look at what to do with them.

_____ Hate

_____ Ungodly music

_____ Pride

_____ Unforgiveness

_____ Alcohol

_____ Gossip

_____ Foul language

_____ Cigarettes

_____ "Don't care" mindset

_____ Ungodly movies

_____ Disrespect

_____ Laziness

_____ Lust

_____ Premarital sex

_____ Other

Everybody deals with something. So if you are going to live a pure life, be honest with yourself and admit what it is that you deal with. Think of what is in your life that you would not want Jesus to know about (as if that were possible). When you admit to an issue, it is easier to move on and change. *Remember that God never expects you to be perfect.* It's true. God knows that you will still sin, even after giving your heart to Him. But think about this saying: **It's not about perfection but direction.** He wants your life to stay moving in the right direction. So when you mess up, get up, ask for forgiveness, and move on in your walk with God.

When it comes to sin, He cares so much about you and the things you face that He mentions them in His Word. These verses aren't here to make you feel bad. They are listed so that you can recognize sin and understand how to live. Let's take a look at what Scripture has to say.

Hate

"Get rid of all bitterness, rage and anger, brawling and slander, along with every form of malice. Be kind and compassionate to one another, forgiving each other, just as in Christ God forgave you."
—Ephesians 4:31–32

Ungodly music

"For you were once darkness, but now you are light in the Lord. Live as children of light (for the fruit of the light consists in all goodness, righteousness and truth) and find out what pleases the Lord."
—Ephesians 5:8–10

Pride

"A man's pride brings him low, but a man of lowly spirit gains honor."
—Proverbs 29:23

Unforgiveness
"And when you stand praying, if you hold anything against anyone, forgive him, so that your Father in heaven may forgive your sins."
—Mark 11:25

Alcohol
"Do not get drunk on wine, which leads to debauchery. Instead, be filled with the Spirit."
—Ephesians 5:18

Gossip
"A gossip betrays a confidence; so avoid a man who talks too much."
—Proverbs 20:19

Foul language
"Out of the same mouth come praise and cursing. My brothers, this should not be. Can both fresh water and salt water flow from the same spring?"
—James 3:10–11

Cigarettes
"Do you not know that your body is a temple of the Holy Spirit, who is in you, whom you have received from God? You are not your own."
—1 Corinthians 6:19

"Don't care" mindset
"For we are God's workmanship, created in Christ Jesus to do good works, which God prepared in advance for us to do."
—Ephesians 2:10

Ungodly movies
"Do not conform any longer to the pattern of this world, but be transformed by the renewing of your mind."
—Romans 12:2

Disrespect
"Show proper respect to everyone: Love the brotherhood of believers, fear God, honor the king."
—1 Peter 2:17

Laziness
"Lazy hands make a man poor, but diligent hands bring wealth."
—Proverbs 10:4

Lust
"For everything in the world—the cravings of sinful man, the lust of his eyes and the boasting of what he has and does—comes not from the Father but from the world. The world and its desires pass away, but the man who does the will of God lives forever."
—1 John 2:16–17

Premarital sex
"Flee from sexual immorality. All other sins a man commits are outside his body, but he who sins sexually sins against his own body."
—1 Corinthians 6:18

Did you allow those verses to sink in your heart, or did you read through them quickly? If you read quickly, go back and take time to think about God's Word. By doing this, you will be strengthened to overcome whatever area is hard for you. Pray these verses when you are tempted. God's Word will help you in those times, and Scripture says so. The psalmist wrote in Psalm 119:11, "I have hidden your word in my heart that I might not sin against you."

God is aware of the temptations in the world. He also allows a way out of them. It's true. Someone once shared a verse with me that changed my whole view on temptation.

Listen to this: "No temptation has seized you except what is common to man. And God is faithful; he will not let you be tempted beyond what you can bear. But when you are tempted, he will also provide a way out so that you can stand up under it" (1 Corinthians 10:13). That is awesome. God will be your strength and courage. If you will give Him whatever it is that is keeping you from living purely, He will carry the burden for you.

Here's What Happened

For me, the whole "give up your burden to the Lord" concept became real when I was sixteen. I was attending a Christian sports camp called Kanakuk Kamp in the woods of Missouri. I was having a great week being involved in activities and meeting new people. But the best part by far was a devotional time held around a campfire that shed its light on a cross. Everyone in the circle was told to think of an area that kept him or her from knowing God and being the best for Him. At that point, we were to write it down and then we would give it to God in prayer.

But instead of just leaving me to pray privately, my counselor handed me a hammer and nail and told me to nail the paper that I had written my burden on to the cross in front of the fire. In tears, I slowly walked toward the cross and placed my sheet of paper at the foot of the wood as if to lay my burden at Jesus' feet. With every hit on the nail I could feel another burden being lifted by Jesus. That was an amazing night, and I have not been the same since.

Here's What Can Happen to You

You can do the same. You don't have to literally nail it to a cross. Just decide to leave that sin behind in your life with Christ—repent and commit to stop doing it—and then strive every day to walk with Jesus. Talk and pray with a friend or youth pastor. Telling them your decision to walk away from a sin will help keep you accountable. You could even ask them to help keep you focused by checking up on that area or talking with you about your growth in God. Any way you look at it, you can do it.

In fact, let's say a prayer together to get you going on the right road, okay? Pray this prayer or one of your own: "God, I know I haven't been the best for You. I have done things that I know were wrong, and I am asking for forgiveness. Please forgive me for not living totally for You, even though You died and rose from the grave for me. I love You, and I want to have a clean slate. Help me to overcome [name sin]. Use me and help me to honor You with my life. Amen."

Well, sister, there you go. You have taken the important first steps to get you going in your life of higher standards. Now that you got some issues out of the way, you are on your way to bigger and better things for God's kingdom!

You're Pretty Cool

Okay, girl, I respect you. You have almost made it to the end of this chapter. That means you have done some serious evaluation of your life. It also means you have been open to some change. That's awesome. The more you choose to live your life 100% for God, the more He is going to reward you in return. Cool stuff is on the way and it is just the beginning.

Just don't forget, the only way to make a difference is by *being different*. Being on track in your relationship with God is the best way to raise the standard. You can be a young woman who will fight to raise the standard and bring others with you. All around you, people are choosing the easier path. You can be the one who is an example for them. That is what *A Girl's Life With God* is all about. It's about you choosing God's way instead of the world's way.

The good news is that you are not alone. As you have accepted Jesus into your life as your personal Savior, He is with you every step of the way. He is walking closer than you can imagine. And if you'll let Him, He will lead you and hold your hand as you go. Pretty cool, huh? Jesus even goes farther in His love for you. He will carry any and every burden you face. That means in all areas, every day. Wow!

Will you always have it easy? No way. But the times when you choose to be different by choosing God are the times your peers (and you) will respect you the most. Be a light that outshines the darkness! Make a change *today*!

 **Speak Up** _____

I want to be different than the world around me because

The area I need to work on the most is

I am going to be an example to my friends by (ex. Not going to certain movies or hanging out with the wrong crowd)

Having Jesus as my number one priority is important because

Even when it is hard, I want to do my best to lead the way for my generation.

____ Yes   ____ No

2

Attitude

Optimistic attitude affects everything.

Dear Journal,
Today was an okay day. Well, everything was going fine until Ashley walked into third hour class. She had the worst attitude. I guess it's nothing new, though. She has an attitude every day. She always has something to complain about, and I can't remember her ever smiling. Her language is horrible, too! Between complaints all I hear are nasty words. I've never really talked to her, except once I told her to "get over it" when she couldn't take a joke from Brian. Other people have tried to talk to her, but she was too busy flinging her hair and looking in the mirror to notice. The more I think about her the worse I feel. Why does she have to be that way? She gets on my nerves. If she would stop being so selfish she might actually enjoy life. I'm so sick of her.

—McKenzie

*E*ver felt like McKenzie after being around someone with a bad attitude like Ashley? People with attitude problems aren't hard to spot. Look around you at school, work, or home. Face it. A bad attitude can be seen virtually anywhere.

McKenzie has a point in this journal entry. Someone like Ashley can be annoying. But something else stands out about McKenzie that she doesn't even realize. She is beginning to develop her own bad attitude! She has allowed herself to be so caught up in the actions of Ashley that she has forgotten what her true responsibility is— her own actions.

Apply this thought of true responsibility to your own life. Since you are striving to lead the way in your walk with Christ, you can't let everyone else affect your goal of being souled out for Christ. This doesn't mean you have to be weird or serious all the time. You have to decide to not act like everyone else as you decide to guard your actions and your attitude when faced with difficult or bothersome circumstances.

How People Can Be

One time I was in line at Barnes & Noble Café (try their iced coffee specialties . . . yummy!), and the woman in front of me went crazy because she was given the wrong amount of change. She was so loud, and people stopped what they were doing to watch the woman spout off a bad attitude. There was so much tension in the air just because one person lacked control. How embarrassing. If she had only known what she looked like.

You will never be able to control every situation in life. There will be people who will bother you. One of my weaknesses is that I get frustrated with people who do things I think are wrong. But I had to learn that I have no right to control others. I don't have to agree with them, but I sure can't let them get the best of me.

Just as I learned, it is not our responsibility to change them, but it is our responsibility to watch how we respond to them. God's Word says in Philippians 2:5,

"Your attitude should be the same as that as of Christ Jesus." And as much as I wish it did, the verse does not say, "Make sure other people have the same attitude as that of Christ." The focus is not on others, but on you (or me).

If I had watched the lady in line at Barnes and Noble, rolled my eyes, shook my head, and then said, "Lady, you're getting on my nerves. Chill out," I would have drawn attention to myself and created my own scene with another bad attitude. People will notice your attitude just as much as you notice others' attitudes.

I remember once I was attending a state pageant in order to judge a portion of the competition. I happened to be on the elevator when a teen and her mom stepped on. I wasn't wearing a banner or nice outfit. I was just kind of bumming until I had to get ready. They had no idea I was a judge. I smiled and said, "Hello," but that was it. The mom smiled back but the girl didn't even respond. She had her arms folded and a look that screamed, "I'm mad at the world!"

Before we got off the elevator, the mom told her daughter that she needed to hold her shoulders back. That's when the girl lost it. She told her mom that she was sick of all that the mom was making her do to get ready for the pageant. She went on to say that she didn't need her mom because she had things under control. That was a bummer to watch. I bet it was even more of a bummer to the girl when she opened the program book and saw I was one of the judges. I hated it for her.

You never know who is paying attention to you! And more than that, you can't allow circumstances to control how you act. That is why a good attitude is a decision you make before you are in a situation. It is a choice that no matter what is going on you have already determined to keep your cool. You have already prepared yourself to be stable.

Talk the Walk

Let's look at how words play a major role in having a good attitude. Has anyone ever said something that really made a difference in your life? Maybe they told you to believe in yourself or to never stop dreaming. Or perhaps they told you that you are beautiful or that you are a compassionate person. Words are powerful and can change our entire perspective about ourselves, our lives, or even about God. You just can't go wrong with positive words.

Take for instance Dr. Neil Smith. He was the head principal at my school, and he was always happy. He walked around singing and always had a smile on his face. Everyday he would tell us to "uplift one another." He took pride in his students and was big on encouraging everyone. After hearing him day after day, I began to catch on to his spirit. One day I decided to make it my goal to be the most uplifting person in the whole school. It felt fantastic! When I saw someone sad or alone I'd say something to make the person smile, or I'd listen to the person. I can't believe the difference it made. I saw frowns turn to smiles, and people seemed to have a better attitude. Words work wonders. They are powerful.

Think about how words already affect you. The words "I'm sorry" can restore a family, and "I love you" can heal a broken heart. In the same way, words of gossip or negativity are powerful, too. Harsh words tear people down and can tear friendships apart. Proverbs 16:28 says, "A perverse man stirs up dissension, and a gossip separates close friends." What you are saying may be true about a person. But why would you lower yourself to an attitude that destroys people? We have to be careful in what we say to others. You must be careful because many unsaved people are watching you as a Christian. People are watching to see if Christianity is real. Use your tongue to build up people. It is the perfect way to influence someone. And the joy of knowing your words have positive influence is priceless!

In Luke 6:45 we hear Jesus say, "The good man brings good things out of the good stored up in his heart, and the evil man brings evil things out of the evil stored in his heart. For out of the overflow of his heart his mouth speaks." This means that what we say is based on what is in our heart. It's the common knowledge of "garbage in, garbage out." What you put in your heart is what will come out of it. In this verse, we are shown that storing up good will cause us to speak good. The more we know God's wisdom, peace, love, and joy, the more others will hear the things of God come from our mouths. That is the only way our words can be positive. It is accomplished by keeping the heart pure.

Home Sweet Home

One of the toughest places to carry a good attitude is at home. Often being around the same people can lead to a lack of respect or appreciation. It is easy to take family for granted when you feel you know them so well. Maybe you don't like your family. I've heard a lot of teens say, "Oh, you don't understand my family. My parents won't get off my case. I'm always getting blamed for every-thing!" or, " I can't stand my siblings! I wish I were an only child. They are so annoying and are so spoiled."

While no family is perfect, let's take a closer look at what you can do to help things out a little. When you are a teenage girl, I know that the world can feel horrible. Some days it's like there is no way out and you will never make it through your teen years. I certainly felt that way at times. In fact, at least once or twice a month I thought the world was coming to an end. But usually I just needed to cry, talk it out, and journal some prayers! And honestly, I know that a lot of times I exaggerated issues.

You may do the same thing. There may have been something like a time when your dad wouldn't let you go out on a Friday night, so then your friends didn't think you're cool. So you cried, told your mother that she can't possibly make you talk to your dad again, and then played your favorite sad song on your stereo for hours at length, and kept slamming the door. Ever done anything like that? If so, don't worry—it's not totally your fault. There is some room for understanding. Your body and emotions are changing. There is a lot of growing up to do, and the teen years can be rough. But I do believe there are ways things could be handled differently.

Here's What Happened

I found out for myself that things could be handled differently when I was thirteen years old. Mom had picked my brother and me up from school, and I had a bad attitude because my day had been bad. But instead of having the attitude of Christ when my mom told me she didn't like the way I was acting, I talked back to her. She even warned me that I was "walking on thin ice" and I didn't let up. Big mistake. About two miles out from the school, my mom pulled her jeep off to the side of the road and jumped out, mad as fire. She went to open my car door and I got scared and locked it. (Big mistake number two.) My brother even turned around in the front seat and said, "You are in so much trouble!" He couldn't have been more right. My mom started beating on the window and I (of course) unlocked the door. That's when she grabbed me out and spanked me right there on the side of the road, unfortunately when all my friends where passing by. Some high school students even honked their horns . . . and I don't think it was out of support. I was humiliated. It was at that time I figured out that a major attitude adjustment could prevent a lot. It was also the last spanking I received!

Ask Yourself This

How has your attitude at home been lately? Think about

it. How has it been in the last week? Have you talked back or been disrespectful? Slammed doors or rolled eyes? Stomped up and down stairs? If you have, then you probably already know that this type of behavior only increases tension and keeps you from getting anywhere.

So what's a girl to do? Try something with me. Try responding instead of reacting. Basically, don't do what feels natural when you get upset, but give yourself some time and think, think, think. Step back and think through what you are trying to accomplish and what will happen to that goal if you have a bad attitude. Allow yourself time to evaluate the situation and circumstances and apply the "attitude same as Christ" verse. That sounds easy, but you have to think quickly and be ready to use self-control!

Practice Makes Perfect

Let's try a practice round for fun. Here's the situation. You want to go to the mall with a few friends from school. Your mom asks you in a negative tone of voice if Kevin is going along too. You say "yes," but hesitantly because you already know that your mom doesn't think he is a good influence. Sure enough, she says you aren't allowed to go. What would you do?

• Give a death look and say, "Mom, I can't believe you. I never get to do anything I want. You are so judgmental of my friends."

• Whine and say, "Please Mom, you let Sarah and Joey [your sister and brother] do anything. Why don't you like me as much as them? I'm going to ask Dad."

• Beg over and over and then run to your room crying while slamming the door and saying, "You hate me."

Do any of these options sound like you? If so, take a look at the following alternate option on what to do in that situation: "Mom, I know Kevin isn't the greatest guy in the world. But I won't be alone with him. Four other

Christian people are going besides him and me. It might actually be good for him to be around Christians. Theresa and I have been talking to him about God. Maybe he'll see that Christians know how to have a great time."

Now don't lose the point here. I'm not saying that hanging out with someone who does not share in a relationship with God is always okay. As you will see in the next chapter, relationships must be handled carefully. The point in this case is the *attitude* toward the parent. The answer toward the mom reflected respect with a good attitude. This type of response will show *volumes* of maturity to your parents. As in, "Whoa. Our kid is mature. Maybe we can trust her a little more." They will also see a girl who is strong in her faith because she knows to carry the attitude of Jesus. As in, "Wow. Our girl really has been growing in her walk with God. Maybe she can handle more than we think."

Even if you don't get your way, at least your attitude was good and God will honor your maturity. It is all in how you choose to act, what you say, and how you say it. You don't have to get caught up in your emotions. Stay calm and think. Be respectful and maintain a good attitude. God will see your heart and bless you for your efforts.

Here's What Can Happen

Your attitude also has a major way of affecting your own life. It can ruin a day in a single instance. And it seems that it comes up slowly and out of nowhere. Regardless of the reasons, a bad attitude can take away a lot of good things. Take a look at a story about what can happen when circumstances take over and a bad attitude rules.

Five A.M. came way too early on a foggy Tuesday morning. Tara's alarm went off for thirty-five minutes before she heard it. The next thing she knew, it was two hours later. It was already one of those dreadful "out-of-the-ordinary days." Her plan was to get up early so she could study for the big chemistry test, take out the garbage, and perhaps even get to school in time to hang out before the bell rang. She was already way behind schedule.

Hurried, she scampered for some clothes, threw a quick lunch together, grabbed her books, and ran out the door. On her drive to school she tried to relieve stress by playing music. The later it got, the louder the music was turned up. Even though she knew it was dangerous, Tara even let herself go fifteen miles over the speed limit. She thought to herself, "If I don't go faster then I will be tardy for a third time and get detention." Just as she sped things up a little, a police car pulled out from behind a tree and stopped her. She thought to herself, "Oh, this is just great. Mom is going to be so mad at me. I will be grounded forever. Where am I going to get the money to pay for the ticket?" Tara rolled her window down and as soon as the officer was near, she threw an attitude fit. "Why did you have to pull me over? I am already late for school and now this. Thanks a lot. I bet you did it because I'm a teenager. You people think we are all alike. Like we don't have a clue about life. This is just great." The officer was not impressed. He told her that he hadn't planned to give her a ticket. He had planned on giving her a warning. But since she was so disrespectful, he decided to give her a ticket after all. Tara was speechless.

Arriving late to school, Tara ran past the hall monitor with an insincere "Hello." She brooded about how she wasn't prepared for the day. The more she thought about everything, the more her attitude fell. "I would have never overslept if I hadn't stayed up late cleaning my room. And I wouldn't have had to clean it so late at night if dad hadn't made me baby-sit." Tara felt frustration taking over her whole attitude.

Chemistry class came and the test she didn't study for started out with a glimpse of hope but then turned on her. Out of anger, she thought to herself, "I might as well have failed. Who likes this class anyway?" After class it seemed that everyone else had to talk to her about "something important." Everywhere she turned people were bothering her with their problems. She felt so tense and angry that she couldn't think straight. How was she supposed to help others? Suddenly, she turned to her two closest friends and said, "Look, I am having a bad day. Can't you guys just leave me alone?" So her friends left her alone and that made Tara feel even worse.

Finally, the day came to an end. The school bell sounded freedom for the day. That afternoon, she decided that she would bum away the rest of the day and forget about everyone else. That is, until she had to tell her mom about the ticket.

After dinner was the perfect time. Tara asked her mom to come into her room. She began to tell the pattern of her day. Halfway through her story, Tara began to cry. As she reflected on the events that had taken place, she began to see how her attitude had brought on problems. From speeding, to talking back to the police, to hurting her friends, Tara knew she had made some mistakes.

All day she had been negative and self-centered. In her own little world she had expected everything to go her way and when it didn't, it bothered her. Now the only thing that bothered Tara was Tara. She felt heavy on the inside because her attitude had ruined her day. But out of it all she had learned something: attitude affects everything.

Are There Exceptions?

Yes, there are attitude exceptions. What do I mean? It would be wrong to say that there is never an appropriate time to have a tough-minded attitude. There are times when it is okay for you to feel strongly about something and have an attitude that displays your feelings.

What am I talking about? I'm talking about righteous

indignation (or being upset over something wrong) in times of injustice. Now wait a minute, before you get too excited, I don't mean the times when you think your parent or teacher has been unfair. I mean when someone has hurt a child and is never punished, or when hungry people across the world can't afford to keep their families alive. It could be about terrorists who attack innocent people or about wars in the East. There are times when it is right to feel negative toward people or events. In fact, if you didn't feel anything toward circumstances like these, it would probably be considered abnormal.

So what should you do with your feelings when these types of situations come up? I suggest doing three things:

#1 Keep your perspective. Be realistic about the situation, but also be real about the world you live in. It is a sinful world because of the fall of man. It won't be perfect until Christ comes back and takes over.

 # 2 Pray. If you are really moved and grieved about a situation, pray about it. Remember that prayer isn't just a thing to do to help you feel better; it actually changes things. Prayer moves the heart of God.

#3 Trust in the Lord. The Lord knows when you are troubled. Think about how He must feel. He sees all the injustice in the world and even died for people so they wouldn't have to live like that. But sin still happens, and He will help you deal with it. He even said in John 16:33, "I have told you these things, so that in me you may have peace. In this world you will have trouble. But take heart! I have overcome the world." Jesus is in control! When you feel the anger the most, call out to Him to help, and He'll be there.

Attitude Affects Others

As we close this chapter, know that you can influence your own attitude. Do you remember the situation at the beginning of the chapter? McKenzie had an attitude toward Ashley. McKenzie wasn't choosing to raise the standard with her attitude. McKenzie was following the crowd. What good is that? It isn't any good, just immaturity and missed opportunity. McKenzie didn't have to agree with Ashley or even really like her, but if McKenzie had an attitude of love toward Ashley, she could have made a world of difference.

You have a choice every day; you can choose to be consumed with how awful people act and how awful you are treated at times, or you can allow the Lord to help you deal with it. Then you can move past yourself and reach out to help others.

You have a truth and answer for people's hurt and pain in life. The answer is Jesus. But how will people know if you don't reach out? How will they see that life in Christ is joyous if our attitude is as bad as theirs? They won't. That is why attitude is a major way you can be different and set a higher standard.

 **Speak Up**_____

1. A good attitude is important because

2. I can keep others from controlling how I act by

3. My words need to be more

4. My attitude can be more like Christ's by

5. My attitude affects

3
Relationships Part I

Never enter a relationship that doesn't help you serve God better.

Dear Journal,
I cannot believe how cute Robby is! I could spend my life just looking at him! I think he might ask me to homecoming. Well, I don't know for sure, but Rachel overheard him tell Jackson that he was thinking about it. I hope he does. I can just imagine how awesome it would be to be with him. I have no idea what I am going to wear to homecoming. Maybe we can match each other. That is, if he even asks me. I can't wait until school tomorrow!
—Marie

Okay girls, this is it. This is the topic that draws attention like nothing else: *Guys*. They can be attractive and funny or smelly and obnoxious. Either way, there is something about boys that causes us to feel, think, and act differently than we do with girls. Learning about the opposite sex can be exciting. You view boys totally differently in your teen years than when you were a kid. Even if you were one of the girls who always chased guys on the playground, it is still different. When a guy comes into your life whom you feel is more than a friend, someone like a best friend whom you are attracted to, that is a whole new issue. It's a very important and fragile issue that must be handled with great care.

So far, you have been challenged to raise the standard in your personal walk with Christ and in your attitude. Now it's time to see a new way to handle relationships. It can be tough to keep your values high in this area, but it can be done.

Dating

Just the word *date* sounds exciting, but it also could be a little nerve-wracking, too. For me, my first date with my husband, Scotty, had two nerve-wracking events. First of all, while getting ready to meet him, I was so excited that I threw up. And the second thing happened when we first got in the car. He thought we should have a Scripture for the day. I thought that was a great idea, until I heard the verse. He opened his Bible and read Proverbs 27:1: "Do not boast about tomorrow, for you do not know what a day may bring forth." My heart sank. I thought, "He is trying to tell me not to look forward to this relationship working out!" Later, after we were married, I asked him about it. He said, "Oh, no. That's not what I meant. It was just a verse I had read in my devotions. I didn't think about it applying to us that way." Isn't it amazing what a date can do to a person?

Anyway, as fun as it is that someone wants to spend time with you, there is a lot more to dating than just going out with someone. *Dating requires smart choices and control of emotions.* It is way too easy to find yourself in a tough situation if you don't guard every step of the way.

My husband is a youth pastor, and he teaches hundreds of teenagers every year about dating. In fact, his view on dating is one of the main things that attracted me to him. He makes the challenge to take a different perspective when it comes to the opposite sex and dating. The ideas in this next section are taken from his dating series, on the topic of "looking at dating for what it is."

It's time to change your mind. It's time to change your brain in dating relationships and love. If you don't want to fall, don't walk where it's slippery. If you don't want scars that will last forever, then stay away from the crossfire of worldly dating.

The Message *paraphrases Philippians 1:9 by saying, "Learn to love appropriately. You need to use your head and test your feelings so that your love is sincere and intelligent, not sentimental gush." Turn on the television and you will see shows containing sentimental gush. Open a magazine and you will find sentimental gush. Talk to your friends at school and you will find sentimental gush. Your relationships can be filled with what is best. For that to happen, however, there must be a change from one way of thinking to another.*

It's easy to say "Amen" in church, but when you get out you say, "Oh, baby" in the bedroom while parents are away. The change must come in your lifestyle.

Don't learn about your relationships by watching average people in society. The world doesn't teach you how to treat, respect, and give in relationships. We know the things in this world are foolish, but what's even crazier is when you participate in its foolishness. This is why you have to change your mind.

People go along with the choices of this world in dating because of three things:

1. Image. *"How am I viewed?" "How do others see me?" "I'd be cool if I could walk into the room with a guy." "I feel weird when all my friends are with their boyfriends and I'm by myself."*

2. Security. *People believe that when they have a relationship they can feel good about themselves. They change the way they dress, what they talk about, and where they go just so they can feel good. They think it's okay to go further than they want because they have someone who likes them.*

3. Pleasure. *Society promotes what you can get out of relationships. One day your boyfriend says, "I love you. I'd do any-*

thing for you," then the next day he says, "I just don't think it will work out between us." He changes because he doesn't love out of commitment, but out of what he can get.

You can't go through the patterns of image, security, and pleasure while thinking you can stay pure and unharmed. If you choose to follow that path, you will be left with three things:

1. Emotional scars—guilt, shame, loneliness, rejection, and regret.

2. Spiritual scars—you find it hard to worship and pray, and there is distance from God.

3. Physical scars—possibility of pregnancy or sexually transmitted diseases.

Scotty has pointed out the typical three motives of relationships and three results that come from following that pattern. If you raise your level of thinking, you can have wonderful relationships that are guilt-free, genuine, and lasting. *The challenge is to turn your attention from image, security, and pleasure to God's ultimate and individual plan.*

Allow the following (**P-U-R-E**) to give you four ways to change your mind in dating:

Prioritize. God wants you to be close to Him before anything else. The worst move you can make is to let a guy come between you and God. You may not even notice how quickly it happens, but when you find yourself running to your boyfriend instead of to God, your relationship is not in order and will eventually end in disaster. However, when both of you prioritize and put your walks with the Lord first (getting into God's Word, praying, attending church, and staying focused), your relationship will be blessed. Matthew 6:33 says, "But seek first his kingdom and his righteousness, and all these things will be given to you as well."

Use accountability. Whether it is a parent, youth worker, or trusted friend, find someone older who will hold you accountable. *Accountability is responsibility.* An accountability partner should help you stay focused on following God, be honest with you if you have messed up, and help you through tough times in your relationship. Open communion will help you stay on the right track because it allows you to talk about problems and seek out advice. An accountability partner should challenge, confront, love, and encourage. Make sure that your partner is someone who loves God, knows the Bible, and will be up-front with you in all types of situations. When you're honest with someone else (and yourself), your relationships will be healthier.

Remember your standards. You don't have to compromise—ever. What you think, what you wear, and how you act around guys does not have to be compromised to get attention. If you know your standards, you can make the right choices. First Thessalonians 4:3–4 tells us, "It is God's will that you should be sanctified [set apart]: that you should avoid sexual immorality; that each of you should control his own body in a way that is holy and honorable." *You have to decide before you get in the situation.* Think ahead of time about how you would handle a situation that may be uncomfortable. Don't allow yourself to be somewhere that could lead to the temptation to become physical. Even if you are strong in your faith, your body is created to enjoy touch, and it will be hard to stop if you are not guarding where you are. Marriage is the time to enjoy God's gift of intimate touch. It is worth the wait, and you can do it!

Enjoy God's gift of friendship. Guys are not made for you to "check out, go out, and make out" with; they are people who offer wonderful friendships. There are amazing blessings in a clean friendship with the opposite sex. Guys can be a lot of fun and can teach you great things.

God created man and woman for each other. He did it to add balance and friendship so that we may be able to serve Him better in life.

Purity

The word *purity* is often spoken of in the Christian world of relationships; but what exactly does it mean? Well, besides the acronym we just learned, Webster's Dictionary says the word *pure* in all its forms means the following: unmixed, untainted, simple, spotless, faultless, and innocent. So now that the definition is clear, you can apply these adjectives to your life by following God's Word and using your brain.

In a relationship between two unsaved people, there does not seem to be any rules. There may be basic etiquette rules, such as opening a door for the girl or calling someone when you say you will, but as far as being pure, there really aren't any guidelines. It is more a "do what feels good" rule. I'm sure you have noticed what I'm talking about among your own friends, in school, or in your workplace. I sure have. Most people usually end up scarred or hurt, and some girls even end up pregnant.

However, in a relationship between two Christians, there are some guidelines that God has laid out to follow. First of all, let's make something clear: *It's not sinful to be attracted or interested in someone. But God does care about how you go about it.* He created the desire you may have to share your life, but He never intends for you to be disobedient in the process. His rules are not meant to take the "fun" away, but rather to keep you from pain and acquiring a regretful past.

Besides, if you follow the Lord you always win. No, seriously. Think of it this way: if you are meant to be with someone, according to God's will, you eventually will get married and can be physical all you want. But if you aren't meant to be and you are physical, you lose a part of yourself to someone who didn't work out anyway. You gave a part of yourself to someone who won't be your husband. So wait and see what God has for your relationship. You don't have to be physical to get to know someone. And if you are "in love" and "know" you are going to work out—great! As soon as you get married, you can be together all you want. See, you win either way! God will always bless you when you follow Him.

✏ Quiz Time _____

Take this quiz to see where you are in some areas that need to be guarded with purity. Choose from "always," "sometimes," or "never."

• I wear clothes that are too tight or too short, but I like the looks or whistles I get from guys.
___ Always   ___ Sometimes   ___ Never

• I try to get guys' attention by making sexual jokes or making comments about my body.
___ Always   ___ Sometimes   ___ Never

• I find myself thinking about how it would be to have a physical relationship with certain guys.
___ Always   ___ Sometimes   ___ Never

• I believe that it doesn't matter how far you go in a physical relationship as long as you don't go all the way.
___ Always   ___ Sometimes   ___ Never

• I feel that it's okay to read secular magazines about sex and relationships.
___ Always   ___ Sometimes   ___ Never

If your answers are:

Mostly "Always"— Do you really think you're making the best choices when it comes to respecting yourself and God? You are headed in the wrong direction. Start working today on achieving purity from the inside out.

Mostly "Sometimes"— You are walking the line between the right and the wrong road. If you work at it, you can change your focus for the better. If you don't, you'll end up with regrets. But if you do, you will be amazed at the respect you will receive from God, yourself, and other teens.

Mostly "Never"— Keep up the good work! You are headed in the direction of wise choices that will keep you out of tough situations, and God will bless you.

All "Never"— You are incredible! Not only do you have a godly view on relationships now, but also you will benefit from the decisions you are making today later in life and marriage.

Quiz Breakdown

There are a lot of issues that can come out of these quiz questions. So let's break down some of them.

Questions #1 and #2: Clothes and comments. Have you ever met a girl who thought that wearing skimpy clothes was all she needed to get attention? The truth is that this type of girl *will* get attention. But what she doesn't know is that it is the wrong kind of attention. It's the kind that goes as quickly as it comes, causes a loss of respect, and reveals nothing but an insecure girl looking for self-esteem. What a girl wears reveals how she feels about herself. If she is revealing her body, she is showing that she does not respect herself or the Lord, and she will not attract a godly guy.

Guys are very visual. This means that what a girl wears can greatly influence thoughts and actions. Is it right for Christian girls to tempt guys to think things about us in a way that is not pure by wearing revealing clothes? No. We can be beautiful to a Christian guy by caring enough about ourselves (and him) to cover what does not need to be seen until marriage.

Question #3: Thought life. Our thought lives are equally important when it comes to purity. It is not wrong to be faced with a thought that does not honor God, but it is wrong to dwell on it and hold it in your mind. The Bible tells us how to do this in Romans 12:2: "Do not conform any longer to the pattern of this world, but be transformed by the renewing of your mind. Then you will be able to test and approve what God's will is— his good, pleasing and perfect will." When sexual thoughts come into your head, renew your mind by praying or reading Scripture. If you don't, those thoughts could take over your whole thought life.

Question #4: How far is too far? When it comes to how far a Christian couple should go in a physical relationship, many questions seem to be left unanswered. It is impossible to know where to draw the line without the instruction of the Bible. Without the Word, everyone is left up to his or her own opinion of when to stop from going too far. First Corinthians 6 contains great insight on how to conduct oneself sexually.

"The body is not meant for sexual immorality, but for the Lord, and the Lord for the body. . . . Do you not know that your bodies are members of Christ himself? Shall I then take the members of Christ and unite them with a prostitute? Never! . . . Flee from sexual immorality. All other sins a man commits are outside his body, but he who sins sexually sins against his own body. Do you not know that your body is a temple of the Holy Spirit, who is in you, whom you have received from God? You are not your own; you were bought with a price. Therefore honor God with your body" —1 Corinthians 6:13, 15, 18–20

So the answer to "How far?" is *none*. Nada. Don't do anything that will set you up for more temptation and will dishonor the body God gave you for a future mate.

It's like this: the Scriptures are providing the guidelines and truths that you are to follow. When you accepted Jesus, you became God's child. You are no longer your own, but you belong to God. That means you should conduct yourself in a way that honors Him. So how does this principle show you how far is too far? *It shows that it's not how far you can go but rather it's how close to God you can stay.*

You are to "flee from sexual immorality." Perhaps holding hands is not immoral, but it is the beginning of what could lead to sin. Typically holding hands turns into hugging, and then hugging to kissing, and then on to moving the hands over the other person's body, and then lying down. The rest of where the process leads is a no-brainer.

The urge to do those things is God-given; however, God gave those feelings for marriage. What you are facing now is the hard part. Controlling the urge to do something you want takes discipline and a heart chasing purity.

So am I suggesting that in order to raise the standard you must not hold hands? Not necessarily. What I am suggesting is that you understand where you could be led to as a physical relationship matures. Be on your guard.

When Scotty and I were dating, we made a rule not to be in a house by ourselves. It wasn't always easy, but it was worth it. There are decisions like that, which you need to think about and make rules for before you even go out with someone. Don't put yourself in awkward positions that leave room for more temptation.

Most of all, if you are in a relationship, pray and ask the Lord to help you be careful and honor Him with your actions. He will be there and *it can be done.*

Question #5: Magazines. In looking at this challenge of guarding how you are with guys, there is a specific area that can break down your sensitivity. It is the area of magazines. All through middle school I read secular teen magazines. But eventually I realized that the information I was reading was totally against God's Word. I thought it was cool to know the latest scoop, but in reality the magazines were tearing me down and giving me a distorted view of relationships.

It's not that looking at all the articles, hairstyles, or clothes are sinful. It's just that there is more harm in a secular teen magazine than there is good. The advice given is typically not from a godly man or woman. If you and I listen to their words, we are opening ourselves up to following the standards of the world. This is not only true for magazines, but also for many other areas of media such as movies, music, advertising, and the Internet.

In order to show you what I mean, I have laid out the differences between the world's advice versus the Bible's. Remember, God's way is not made to be boring, it's made to give you the best in life. Here are some examples of the differences:

• *It's okay to go too far physically if you are in love.*
1 Thessalonians 4:3— "It is God's will that you should be sanctified: that you should avoid sexual immorality."

• *If a guy is a jerk, talk about him behind his back.*
Proverbs 21:23— "He who guards his mouth and his tongue keeps himself from calamity."

• *Girls who dress immodestly are cool.*
Proverbs 31:30— "Charm is deceptive, and beauty is fleeting; but a woman who fears the LORD is to be praised."

• *It's okay to lust after guys.*
Philippians 4:8— "Whatever is true, whatever is noble,

whatever is right, whatever is pure, whatever is lovely, whatever is admirable . . . think about such things."

• *Being loved by a boy is the ultimate love.*
John 3:16— "For God so loved the world that he gave his one and only Son, that whoever believes in him shall not perish but have eternal life."

Do you see the differences in the standards of the world and God's standards? When you read secular magazines or allow certain media to capture your attention, it is easy to get caught up in the low values and think that is the way it should be. Don't be deceived. Use your head when it comes to choosing what you read, watch, and listen to because what goes in the head becomes a part of your heart, and then flows out into your actions.

Don't Forget Forgiveness
In this chapter we have covered a lot of stuff. Some of these thoughts you may want to read over again, just to let them sink in. As you evaluate and perhaps change some things you are doing in relationships, don't forget forgiveness.

If you have read this chapter and feel discouraged because you have gone past the standards represented, it is not too late for you to start again. If you have made decisions such as losing your virginity, getting pregnant, having an abortion, or contracting an STD, God can heal your past. Daniel 9:9 says, "The Lord our God is merciful and forgiving, even though we have rebelled against him." 1 John 1:9 also says, "If we confess our sins, he is faithful and just and will forgive us our sins and purify us from all unrighteousness."

Closing Prayer

Overall, I believe we've covered some deep topics in this chapter. Since I can only touch on so many areas, I understand that you will probably face other situations and problems. Just remember the principle at the beginning of the chapter: *Never enter a relationship that doesn't help you serve God better.* As you face new circumstances, memorize this prayer and let it be a reminder to you of your choice to rise up when it comes to relationships:

Dear God,
I know that I am created as Your daughter. You have so many great plans for my life, even in relationships. I want to follow in Your ways of purity. Keep me from following the patterns of the world that do not honor You or myself. I trust that as long as I am doing my best to be pure, You will take care of my desires and dreams. I give it all to You and Your timing.

🖘 Speak Up

1. My view of guys could change by

2. I can make sure I am doing my best to stay pure by

3. There are some magazine articles that I need to stop reading. ___ Yes ___ No
Such as

4. Dating can be honoring to God by

5. If God intends for me to marry, I know He has a godly man just for me! ___ Yes

4
Relationships Part II

*Treat people right: Relationships are the only
things you can take to heaven.*

Dear Journal,
Today was crazy. Cari told me that the new girl in
our gym class thinks I'm a snob. I didn't mean to
come across as snobby. I just thought I wouldn't be
as outgoing as I usually am because last time
there was a new girl she said I was "overbearing."
Sheesh! How can I win? Besides that, my family is
weirding out on me. I have a brother who thrives
on doing anything rebellious, a little sister who is
obsessed with being with me 24/7, a dad who is
having to work overtime all the time, and a mom
who seems stressed with all of us and with
Grandma's cancer. I love my family, but sometimes
it is hard to communicate with them. I think I
need a major vacation getaway by myself!
—Hailey

*D*id any of the above journal entry sound familiar to
you? Have you ever felt overwhelmed with the relationships around you? If you are a teenage girl (or anyone
else for that matter), you have faced times of stress with
friends and family. Relationship trials are inevitable,

which means they are going to happen. And I bet you could tell me a million friendship stories just off of one year (or maybe month, week, day?!) of school!

Since there are going to be difficult times with the people you love, it will help you to know how to handle them. It is especially important in your Christian walk. Why? As a Christian girl, you should handle things differently than the average unsaved person does. People are going to hurt you, disappoint you, and frustrate you; but you can overcome those things. It won't be easy—it will take some serious maturity. But if you are taking the challenge of this book and saying you want to raise the standard of Christian teens, I believe you can master this chapter too!

Part I—Friends

Friends are gifts from God. There's nothing like a late night of girl friends hanging out in their PJs, watching a movie, and eating snacks! I can remember a night when my friends Natasha and Stephanie were staying over. We were in mid-high school, but we had a blast acting like little kids! We turned on music from a theater production and we danced around and pretended we were in the play. It went on for a couple of hours! My mom happened to walk in on us, and she laughed hysterically at the fun we were having. She even got out the video camera. That night was definitely a night I won't forget. I have had some wonderful friends through the years.

The memories that you have with your friends are probably just as special to you. You may have dozens of friends, a few friends, or one best friend. It doesn't matter how many you have, just that you understand the value your friends. If you have ever been without a friend, it is easier to know the worth of a friend when you do have one. So let's talk about how to handle these valuable people in friendships.

Making a Friend: How

Some girls who are reading this book are thinking, "I don't even have a single friend to value." And for various reasons, they truly may not have even one friend. If that describes you, chill. It's okay. Most everyone has felt that way at some point. Sometimes we are without friends because of a move, a change of churches, or perhaps because we aren't sure how to be a friend. Whatever the case, you *can* make friends.

I have been without a friend on several occasions. There were times I went to camp and didn't know a single person. There were times I visited churches and I didn't know anyone. And there were times when I had to change schools and I didn't know anyone. My family moved to four different states when I was growing up. That wasn't always easy. Every time, I had to reestablish new friendships.

I remember my first day at a new school when I was in first grade. There were only two months of school left, and everyone had already picked their friends. My teacher tried to help me adjust to the new class, but everyone just looked at me. That is, except for one girl. She had long black hair and huge dimples. She smiled at me and invited me over to play. I was thrilled! I didn't know what to do or say, but I let her show me how the toys worked. Then she saw my watch and asked if I knew how to read it (it had hands and numbers). When I told her I could, she thought that was so cool. We hit it off and have stayed best friends every since. Even after I moved again, we have been close. We were in each other's weddings as the maid of honor, we call and fly out to see each other, and we will always be there for each other.

So how do you make a friend? Proverbs tells us all we need to know. It says we must be friendly in order to make a friend. You may be thinking, "That's it? I've heard that tons of times." Even if you have heard that over and over, it is the truth. If you want a new friend, go out and be a friend. If you don't and you wait for someone to come to you, you may be waiting a long time. Or if someone has already approached you and you aren't a friend back to her, you won't keep her as a new friend.

There is a girl I know who is always by herself. She won't get involved in the youth activities, and if you talk to her she acts like she doesn't care. What amazed me is that her parents came to me and said that they wished their daughter fit in at church. I hated to admit it, but their daughter would fit in at church if she allowed herself to be a friend back to all the girls who are trying to be her friend. All she has to do is start thinking of other people instead of herself. If she acted interested in someone else, she could have many friends.

And what if you have been a friend but the other person isn't responding? You should talk to them and ask them what is up. Maybe they really do want you as a friend but they are going through a hard time. You may be just what they need. Or if you have tried to be a friend and things aren't clicking for the two of you, move on. It's okay to admit things aren't working out. God may have another person that would be better for you to be close to. Just be open.

Making a Friend: Who

Now that you know that you have to be a friend to have a friend, let's talk about whom you should have as friends. Already you may be thinking, "I can have anyone I want as a friend. It's my life! You're not my mom." Well, you are right about one part—I am not your mom, but the rest of that thought you may need to reconsider. It's what my mom calls "stinking thinking." So before you let this way of thinking go too far, remember that this book is about you changing the way you live. If you want to be an average Christian girl, you can do that. But if you want to be different and make a difference, keep reading about how your friends are totally important.

Your friends represent who you are. Like it or not, if you choose people who love God and are living for Him, it is a good sign of what you love and are living for. Whereas if your friends drink, watch bad movies, and wear skimpy clothes, you are with the wrong people. Who you choose to spend your time with represents what is in your heart.

The Bible even talks about who should be your friend. Second Corinthians 6:14–15 says, "Do not be yoked together with unbelievers. For what do righteousness and wickedness have in common? Or what fellowship can light have with darkness? What harmony is there between Christ and Belial [Satan]? What does a believer have in common with an unbeliever?" And James 4:4 says, "You adulterous people, don't you know that friendship with the world is hatred toward God? Anyone who chooses to be a friend of the world becomes an enemy of God." What awesome verses to remember when it comes to choosing whom you hang out with. They totally make sense.

Think about it this way. What if your friend said, "I am going to wear a jersey with my school name and colors on it, but I am going to go sit on the rival team's bench and cheer for them"? Would that be weird or what? Why would anyone claim to be for one team but interact and cheer on another team? What would they have in common? Why would you fellowship with someone who is not for the team you are for?

It works the same way with choosing your friends. The friends that you are always hanging out with or wanting to be with shouldn't be unbelievers. Is it wrong to have acquaintances or surface friends who don't know God? Absolutely not. You are probably the biggest impact in their life and they may come to know Christ because of you. However, there is a difference in reaching someone for God and including them so that they may accept

Christ versus having friends that you love to be with who are away from God and do things you know aren't best. Be smart about who you allow to impact you.

Being a Friend

Once you have chosen and made friends, it helps to know how to keep them. It would be a bummer to choose the person and be friendly and then lose them because you weren't sure how to keep them. Friendships take time and love.

I came across a book called *Encouraging People* that was written back in the late eighties by Donald Bubna. Even though the book most likely came out while you were little or not even born yet, the principles are great and totally apply to you today. There are five qualities that the author believes are characteristics of a friend:

#1. A friend is accessible. This means that you are available to your friends. If your friend needs to talk or work through something, you are there for them. Even if they can't get to you in person, they know they can always email, call, or write.

#2. A friend builds bridges. This means that you are willing to work through differences. If there is a problem, you do your best to correct it. You are a peacemaker. This is an especially good quality when it comes to having two friends who are fighting with each other. You can build a bridge between them and help them get through their differences.

#3. A friend is consistent. This means that you don't change. Your friends don't wonder if you are going to talk to them or be nice to them—they know you will. They won't feel used because you only hang out with them when there is no one else. If you are consistent, you will be a friend who doesn't change based on circumstances.

#4. A friend wants her friend to succeed. This means that you truly want to see your friends have good things happen. If they get a new outfit, you aren't jealous. If they make the team and you don't, you aren't mean and angry. It also means that you try to help them succeed. Maybe you could help with a science project or catch their basketball rebounds, or drop them a note and tell them that you are praying that God would bless them.

#5. A friend is generous with her resources. This means that you are a giver. Whatever you have, you share. You can give a friend time, gifts, encouragement, or even a listening ear. If you give of what you have, you will get in return a wonderful friend who loves and appreciates you.

These five qualities are cool ways you can keep the people you love around as friends for life. Just do the golden rule from Luke 6:31, which says, "Do to others as you would have them do to you." And above all, love your friends at all times. Even when your friend makes a bad decision or goes through a hard time, be there for them. Proverbs 17:17 says it this way: "A friend loves at all times, and a brother is born for adversity." That means no matter what—love your friends!

Confronting a Friend

Have you ever had a friend who claimed to be a Christian but then she did some things that you knew were wrong? Have you ever felt like your friend treated you wrongly and hurt you? If so, then you understand how hard it is to deal with something like that. It can be tough to know if you should say something or just let her figure it out on her own. It can be hard to wait and see if she notices that she has offended you. And it can be even harder to know you should say something but not know how to do it. But guess what? Scripture once again can help. Matthew 18:15–17 tells you how to handle a friend who has hurt you or is hurting herself. It says:

"If your brother sins against you, go and show him his fault, just between the two of you. If he listens to you, you have won your brother over. But if he will not listen, take one or two others along, so that 'every matter may be established by the testimony of two or three witnesses.' If he refuses to listen to them, tell it to the church; and if he refuses to listen even to the church, treat him as you would a pagan or a tax collector." —Matthew 18:15–17

So what is all of that saying to you today? Let's talk it through. Here are the basic steps. First, if you have been hurt or if a "brother," meaning another Christian, is living in sin, go and talk to her about it. Tell her what is on your heart. If she has said something that hurt you, let her know. If she is doing something that you both know is wrong, bring the matter up. But remember that the verse says that you should go alone. Yeah, I know, a teenage girl going alone to talk about something big isn't easy. It's even sometimes more fun to get other friends involved and active in confronting someone. But that isn't good. It will make things worse.

Before you go, *make sure your goal is to do it in love.* If you go to her with an attitude or while you are angry, she probably won't listen to you. And give her time. Most people are defensive when they are first confronted. That doesn't mean that she won't apologize or change. She may just need some time to think and deal with it.

I know all of this is easier to say than to do. Confrontation is not and should not be fun. (If it is fun to you, you may wan to check your heart and motives.) But what are your options? You can be hurt for the rest of your life and your friend may continue to sin, or you can have the courage to say something and solve it and help her before it is too late. Be bold and go to her. The Scripture above says that if she listens to you—great! You have done the right thing and she has accepted your comments!

Secondly, if you go to her in love and confront her and she won't change, you should take a friend or two with you and talk with her again. This time it's okay to take someone with you. I wouldn't choose just anyone, though. Make sure the person or people you take understand how you are approaching the issue. That way, they can make sure they walk in love too.

Thirdly, if the friend has not listened to you by then, you should go to a trusted spiritual leader. At that point you tell them what happened and how you have handled it. Then let them talk with the friend.

Finally, if at this point the person does not respond, you should cut off that relationship. That can be hard. But by now, you probably have figured out that the friend doesn't care about you or about the sin. I hope you never have a friend who reaches this point. But if she does, let her go. You have done all that you were supposed to do in order to win her back. Maybe you can tell her that you still love her and will pray for her. You may even tell her that when she is ready to change you will be glad to be her friend again.

Part II—Family

Growing up, I used to watch a show on TV called *Family Matters*. I think it was one of the best shows that has ever been created. In the Winslow family there was a mom and dad, three kids, an aunt and nephew, and a grandmother who all lived in the same house. Then there was Erkle, the nerd next door, who practically lived at the Winslows'. Every show showed how the family faced things that were everyday trials and family issues. The episodes always ended in love and the problems were resolved.

Don't you wish that real life could be that way? I sure do. I would love to have all the problems or trials in my family solved in thirty minutes and have everyone hug at the end! That doesn't always happen in the real world, but it *is* a model that you can strive to follow. I know you can't write the "script" of everyone else's role, but you can control your part in your family. It's all in how you view your family, find your family, and love your family.

Viewing Your Family: As People

It's weird how one day life can be viewed one way, and the next day it changes completely. A couple of years ago I left my teens and entered my twenties. In that time I got married, graduated college, joined my husband's ministry as a pastor's wife, worked as a writer, and had a baby. In the last three years I have learned a lot and have grown a lot.

One of the biggest things I have learned in this time is that my parents are actually *people*. That sounds funny, doesn't it? But growing up I didn't think of my parents as two people who grew up in their own family and had their own lives before they got married and I came around. I usually just saw them as "Dad" and "Mom," and they were supposed to have life all figured out. Now that *I'm* the "Mom," I see things as they truly are—we are all people who are learning and growing. I would often get upset at my parents because of the way they would handle something or do something. But now I know that they were working hard and doing their best.

I think that how you view your family will help in how you deal with them. Your family is made up of people who are struggling through life just like you are. For example, if your brother is not living for God, instead of viewing him as a jerk and hypocrite, think of him as a person wrestling with his faith. He is deciding who he will follow—the world or God. If your parents are going through some times of fighting, try to view them as two people who are working through some personal problems and some relationship problems. This will make it easier to understand how they are feeling rather than telling yourself over and over how you wish they would get their act together. Your family faces trials just like you do. Their trials may be on a different level and about different things, but trials are trials and everyone has them. I'm not saying that you have to be happy about your parent's divorce or excited that your brother isn't living for God. I'm just suggesting that you view your family members as people who are on the same journey of life as you are. And sometimes the journey can be tough!

Viewing Your Family: The Purpose

Every person born is part of a family. Profound, huh? I bet you have already thought of that before! But have you ever asked yourself what is the purpose of family? Have you thought about why God places people automatically into a certain group of people? God started the family in the Garden of Eden. That was before He started the church! And God refers to His relationship with Jesus as a father-and-son relationship. And He even talks to Christians as we are a part of the family of God. We are considered "brothers" and "sisters" in faith. God is big on the family.

I think He loves the family because He knew we all needed a place to belong. He knew that we would need other people. People need to sense that they are a part of a people group. Family gives a person a heritage and a foundation. Family gives us people we can count on, celebrate life with, and face hard times with. Everyone needs a family.

Finding Your Family

So what about the people who don't have a family? What about the girls who have lost their parents, have never seen their brothers or sisters, have been kicked out and rejected, or have been taken away because of circumstances?

There is good news! There is still a way to be a part of a family!

Psalm 27:10 says one of the coolest things in the world: "Though my father and mother forsake me, the LORD will receive me." Let's put that in today's words: Though my family has fallen apart and I feel lonely and rejected, God loves me and will take care of me. Basically, if you feel like you don't have a family, you can be in the family of God. He is the best Father you can find, and He will take care of His children. His Word even says in Philippians 4:19, "And my God will meet all your needs according to his glorious riches in Christ Jesus."

If you hear that and still think, "That's good, but I want a physical family that I can talk to about life and go to on the holidays!" it's okay. If you are a part of God's family and you are living for Him, He will send people into your life to be your family. There is a young girl in our church who doesn't have a family, but God provided a couple who took her in and has been a family to her. Family doesn't have to be blood-kin related people. A family can be anyone God sends to help you and love you. That's a true family!

Loving Your Family

Since everyone has the opportunity to be a part of a family, whether it is by relative blood or Jesus' blood, it helps to know how to love them. This can be difficult because sometimes family can become so close that it's hard to be nice, much less love them! But there are three things you can do to show love to the people in your life.

• **Be a helper.** You are an important part in your family. No one else can be you. Your family needs you. Yep. Hard to believe? It's true. Your family needs you to help them, just as you need them to help you. How? You can help in the little things like chores or errands, or in the big things like encouraging and listening when others are down. Just remember you are not the only one in your family. There are others who need *you!*

• **Pray for them.** As you know, families can face many things together. Death, divorce, addictions, abuse, sickness, and moral conflicts are just a few things that can hit a family. So what can you do? You can do all that you need to do—pray. Psalm 34:17 says, "The righteous cry out, and the LORD hears them; he delivers them from all their troubles." When you are discouraged about your family or in a place where the situation is out of your control, prayer is all you need. It works miracles!

• **Be a peacemaker.** One of the greatest ways to love your family is to be part of the blessings, not part of the problems. Your attitude and actions can make a world of difference in your home. Go with the old "peace out" saying! Be a peacemaker, not a peace breaker! Romans 12:18 puts it this way: "If it is possible, as far as it depends on you, live at peace with everyone." Let's say that you are having dinner with your family and your parents start to argue, then your little sister drops and breaks her plate by accident, and the dog starts barking. What could you do in that situation? I know what I would want to do. I would want to roll my eyes, put my hands over my ears, and leave the room while saying, "I can't take it anymore!" But this wouldn't be being a peacemaker. What you could do is let your parents solve their own problem, clean up your sister's mess and tell her it's okay, and let the dog out. Now that would be some peace signs!

Closing Thoughts

I hope you have enjoyed this chapter. Friends and family are important. I respect you for desiring to be above average in your relationships with the people you love. Do what you can, and people who love to hang out with you and call you their family will surround you!

Speak Up _____

1. One thing that would help me make friends would be

2. My current friends are (good) or (not good) because

3. When it comes to being a friend, I could be better at

4. If I would _____, I would get along better with my family.

5. One way I can love my family is by

Body Wise

*Take care of yourself,
but learn to accept yourself as God made you.*

Dear Journal,

Today I felt so fat. I've been working hard on the way I look, but I think I'm getting worse. I hate the way I feel when I sit down—all my stomach rolls. I'll never look pretty because, well . . . I don't know. Just thinking about all this makes me want to eat. Now I feel guilty. I feel trapped inside myself. Nobody knows how I feel. Good night.

—Maddie

This journal entry is an example of the thoughts of a lot of teenage girls. Maddie has truly expressed how she feels about her body and the way she looks.

She does not feel that she is good enough. That is a horrible feeling. The sad truth is that most girls face that feeling often throughout their life. Where do those feelings come from? Perhaps it comes from comparing oneself to other girls. Have you ever noticed how teenagers try to look like someone on TV or on the cover of a magazine? How often do you see girls in real life that match the girls in the media? The answer is probably not very often. The reason for that is there are numerous ways those girls are "touched up" with computers, make-up, and perfect lighting. No wonder it is hard to add up to society's expectations of a "beautiful woman"—most of them aren't revealing their true body! I know this is true because it happened to me. There was a bridal magazine that asked me to do some work for them. I did the pictures, and when the magazine came out my friends said, "Is that you on the front of that magazine? It doesn't even really look like you!" I told them it was me but that I wasn't surprised that the photo didn't look like me. I had spent over two hours having my hair and makeup done. I looked way different than how I actually look!

No one is perfect. That's right, no matter what a girl looks like, there will always be something she wishes she could change. She may be content with her eyes, but if only her smile was better; or maybe a girl has beautiful legs, but her feet are huge. Whatever the case may be, people deal with physical confidence.

Part One: The Outer Person

In this chapter we're going to talk about how you can feel confident with the way you look and feel. First, I want to remind you that the physical aspect of yourself should always come after the spiritual. Proverbs 31:30 says, "Charm is deceitful, and beauty is fleeting; but a woman who fears the Lord is to be praised." The girl on the inside should be the number one focus. In the second half of this chapter we'll talk about this most-important aspect. But for now, while the spiritual part of you should be the primary concern, it is also important to take care of your physical body.

Time Out

When we discuss the physical body, think about taking care of yourself because you are representing the Lord, not because you are out to impress the world. If you are striving for a magnificent body so you can be sexy and wear sexy clothes, watch out! That is dangerous. You are asking for trouble with guys, a poor reputation, and most likely you won't even be comfortable!

You actually can look nice without looking sexy. I know, hard to believe, huh? It's true, though. You can choose to look classy or casual or whatever you want, but if you choose the sexy route, evaluate your motives and see if your heart is pure as to why you would wear certain things. And yes, I know it is hard to shop these days with all the tight clothing and belly-baring styles. But you can always add a sweater or tie something around your waist. And when in major doubt whether your look is too sexy and revealing, ask, "How would I feel if Jesus saw me wearing this?"

Time In

Anyway, back to where we left off. Maddie's journal at the beginning of the chapter describes one of the main insecurities teenagers face—feeling fat. During these years your body is changing so much. You're growing from young ladies into women. This means you are growing above the waist, below the waist, and sometimes at the waist. But this is natural.

Dr. Paul Rothwell from the Christian teen magazine *Brio* agrees. In the October 2000 issue, a girl wrote to his "Ask Dr. Paul" column and asked what the average weight of a 15-year-old girl should be. He starts off by saying, "The answer to this question always gets me in a lot of trouble! As girls go through puberty, it's normal for them to gain weight—and specifically in the hips and thighs. Unfortunately, this happens during a time when girls are very concerned about body image—but it's *normal!*" Wow! Even a doctor says it's normal for you to be changing! If you didn't change, then you would end up being thirty years old in a ten-year-old body! So since you are rapidly changing, what can you do to control your body and maintain confidence?

Well, I don't have all the answers, but I have a couple of ideas that have helped me. I am not a doctor or anything, so before you do anything too drastic, make sure you check with your health professional or let a parent know what's up. Again, these ideas are things that have worked for me as a teenager and even now. So apply it to your life as best fits.

Here's the Plan

1. Decide to look your personal best. Every girl reading this book is designed in her own unique and special way. This is how God planned for you to be created. That is why I can't look like you and you can't look like me. We all have different bodies. What we can do is work with what we have. If you are a size 10 and your best friend is a size 4, odds are you have a different bone structure. Don't starve yourself in order to become something you're not; consider your body type and work from there.

This applies to maintaining a healthy body weight and also to cleanliness. As a teenager, cleanliness is a must. You probably already know that, but some girls don't think about it as often as they should. You don't have to be ready for prom everyday. Just have fun staying groomed. You only have one body, so shower, shave, style, and don't forget those nails! When you are clean, you will feel better about yourself.

2. Move that body! Exercise can help your self-esteem about your body improve dramatically! Not only can it be fun, but also you will release stress and receive a ton of other benefits. And no matter what body type you have, exercise is for everyone.

For smaller girls, you may not need to burn fat, but working out could add shape to your frame. Weight lifting is excellent for adding shape. Or if you're interested in losing weight, begin with some aerobic exercise. This doesn't mean you have to join a health club. It simply means to exercise by walking, biking, swimming, or any other way of consistent movement you enjoy.

Just remember, your body didn't become what it is overnight and it won't change overnight either. Start slowly and work your way into more. For the best results, activity for thirty to forty-five minutes three to four times a week is recommended. The most important thing to remember is that exercise requires discipline and commitment. It's not always easy, but it is always rewarding. You will begin to feel great!

3. Think before you eat. Food is wonderful! There's so much to choose from: Chinese, Italian, Mexican, and good old American. Because of these good choices, it can be hard to choose the food best for you after it's been in your mouth. So when you're about to eat, think first. Does it contain a lot of sugar or is it high in fat? You may think this is no big deal because you are young, but bad diets aid in producing lifelong illnesses over the years such as heart disease, cancer, and obesity.

Now is the best time to develop positive eating habits. You don't have to be over thirty to start having problems. Every day teenagers deal with medical issues as a result of their food choices. When it comes to eating, think moderation and *eat to live, don't live to eat.* Start developing a healthy lifestyle that will last through all your tomorrows.

4. Maintain a healthy mindset. Think of it this way: you are created in the image of God. *He has made you for a reason and gave you the body you have to use for His glory.* If someone gave you a car and said that it was the only one you could have for the rest of your life, wouldn't you take care of it? Of course you would. If you didn't, it would break down and be useless. Think of your body as the only vehicle you have until you die. If you don't watch how it is treated, it may break down and be useless!

Eating Disorders

A few years ago my friend attended an athletic camp. She came back and shared how 75% of the girls in her cabin admitted to having an eating disorder. That's outrageous! This is a major problem. You may know this is true because you have been faced with eating problems.

Some people may condemn teenage girls for their eating problems. They may say that it's just not healthy or right to treat yourself that way. They may talk about how it's just not good to throw up after every meal or that starving yourself is not the answer. They are right, but I also know from a teen's perspective that eating disorders are not something that is asked for. Usually, it starts with something like this: Open magazine. See girl. Study body. Look at self. Think hard. Too fat. Throw up.

Or, maybe it's this: Girl has boyfriend. Boyfriend is cruel. Insults girl. Girl feels insecure. Must look better. Stop eating.

Wherever or however it started, if you aren't sure how to break free from an eating disorder I encourage you to seek help. You can't be an overcomer by your own ability, but through God all things are possible. You are not alone in this battle, and God wants to set you free. Get with your youth pastor or another adult to help guide you in the right way and to pray with you. There are also camps and professional counseling to help, such as Remuda Ranch (www.remudaranch.com). Just do whatever it takes to get out of your addiction. You deserve the best.

Part Two: The Inner Person

Now that we have covered some practical aspects of taking care of the outer girl, let's move on to the true you—the inner girl. Self-esteem, how we views ourselves, is a huge issue among teenage girls. Throughout my time in the ministry, I am asked more about this topic than any other.

Why do you think teens face low self-esteem? Why is it hard for girls to know who they are and be motivated to be something and do something great for the Lord? I don't believe there is a set answer, but I think there are definitely certain things that can detour a girl's confidence. It could be that no one has ever told her she is valuable, or perhaps a life of sin has kept her from feeling worthy of respect.

Although there are many circumstances that could cause negative feelings about yourself, there are also ways to overcome those feelings. No matter what may cause you to doubt your value and potential, you can get out of those thoughts about yourself. You actually can walk in confidence!

Who Will You Listen To?

You have an enemy. His name is Satan. He rules the sinful world and he hates you. He won't ever say he hates you or is out to kill you, but he does and he is, and he'll approach you in subtle ways. He wants you to hate yourself and never feel important. He wants you to drown in self-doubt and pity. He is your worst nightmare!

I bet you're wondering where that came from! Right in the middle of a nice, innocent chapter you were hit with the devil. Here's why. All lies come from Satan. All attacks come from Satan. He is the very opposite of Jesus. John 10:10 says, "The thief [Satan] comes only to steal and kill and destroy; I [Jesus] have come that they may have life, and have it to the full."

I wanted you to be reminded of all that because you have to know where the root of low self-esteem comes from—Satan. To some of you, that may sound weird. Usually it seems that people think of Satan as the one trying to get people to murder, steal, and commit all those kind of sins. But actually, Satan can come against you in many other forms, one of which is the form of self-doubt. Why would he do that? Think about it. If Satan can get you to feel like you aren't worth anything and that you will fail if you step out and try something new, then he has won the battle against God using you in ways to advance the gospel. This can also come in many fashions. Advancing the gospel isn't just going out on the mission field, although low self-esteem could keep someone from doing that, too. Advancing the gospel based on your self-esteem could mean . . .

• That you have the courage to boldly witness to someone in the hallway at school,

• It could mean that you have the confidence to participate in a sport or event that would give you a platform to tell others where your strength comes from,

• Or it could mean that your decisions are not swayed by peer pressure.

After looking at just a few ways that confidence affects your life, it is easy to see why Satan would want to keep you from believing in yourself.

Will You Listen to God?

So now that you know that low self-image is from the enemy, here's what you need to know from God's perspective. This is your ammunition against esteem attacks!

God has a plan for your life. Ephesians 2:10— "For we are God's workmanship, created in Christ Jesus to do good works, which God prepared in advance for us to do." God has incredible goals for your life! How can you accomplish His plan if you lack confidence? Your confidence is in knowing your life is going somewhere because God has things in store for you.

You are not a mistake. Psalms 139:13–14a— "For you [God] created my inmost being; you knit me together in my mother's womb. I praise you because I am fearfully and wonderfully made." You are not here by chance, even if you were born out of your mother being raped or your parents not planning for you. God doesn't make mistakes. He doesn't make a person and then say, "Oops! Oh well. I guess that person will just have to make do in life. I don't have any plans for her." No way! He made you and no one else in the whole world is like you. Which means no one else can fulfill and live the life God has for *you!*

You can do anything. Philippians 4:13— "I can do everything through him who gives me strength." Are you afraid of trying something new? Pray this Scripture! Don't have the confidence to tell your friends "no" to going out to a party or watching an R- rated movie? Pray this Scripture!

Those thoughts are just the beginning of the genuine confidence you can gain. Knowing who you are in the Lord, realizing that there is a call on your life, and allowing God to enable you with His strength—now that's high self-esteem!

Practical Steps

This next section is designed to give you some easy and practical steps to follow as you fight low self-esteem. These are things that worked for me personally. I have used these three steps hundreds of times in my life in many situations when I was faced with low confidence. But you have to know that *the only way these steps work is by knowing your value in the Lord as mentioned in the previous section*. There are many views on how to gain confidence, but the only confidence that lasts is the confidence in the Lord. But as you grow in that confidence in God, perhaps these next steps will help you along the way.

Do things to step out of your comfort zone and let failure bring out the best in you. You have to do things you are afraid of doing! Once you do them you will be amazed at how confident you'll feel! If you fail, learn from your mistakes and grow. Then try again!

I had to step out of my comfort zone when I entered

my first pageant. I was thirteen, with frizzy hair, glasses, braces (that strived to pull my long-spaced two front teeth together), and legs that seemed longer than anyone else's in the whole school district! I was in my awkward stage (which, for those of you still in yours, it only lasted until ninth grade. There's an end to it!).

I saw an advertisement for a local level pageant for girls ages thirteen to seventeen. Even though I would be the youngest, I thought I should enter it. My parents where very concerned. They knew I didn't look people in the eye or smile much. My posture was terrible, and I didn't have any clue how pageants worked. They tried to talk me out of doing it. I remember my dad sitting across from me at the mall saying, "It's just that I don't want you to feel ugly for the rest of your life if you lose." I understood where he was coming from, and deep down I didn't want to feel that way either, but I knew that if I was ever going to learn these skills, I had to go for it.

When I arrived at my first rehearsal, I looked around, evaluated the crowd of girls, looked in the mirror, and thought, "Well . . . maybe I shouldn't be here." Then I found another girl with braces and frizzy hair and made friends with her and decided to stick with it. Two months later, at the night of the crowning, I stood in a light purple $20 thrift store dress and heels I couldn't walk in. The lights were bright and my friends from school were there. I gave it my best. I smiled and tried to hold my head and shoulders back; I thought, *Surely I have placed.* But no. I didn't place. I didn't win. I didn't even get Miss Congeniality.

I went back to the dressing room and my mom came in slow and quiet. I started to cry. She hugged me and said I never had to do another one. Then it hit me. This was my first pageant. I couldn't give up now. Now I knew what to expect and how things worked. I had to try again. And I did. But before I did, I let the event of losing the pageant cause me to learn and grow. I read books about pageants, attended charm classes, and asked a ton of "How can I improve" questions.

At the next pageant, that same year, I placed second runner-up. The next year I won a county title. And it went on from there, five years after that first pageant, as I stood on a stage and accepted a national title.

What if I had never stepped out and tried pageants? What if I had stayed in my comfort zone? What if I hadn't wanted to improve and grow? I would have missed out on tons of incredible experiences! Don't hold back. Get out there and try something new!

Don't let others dictate your worth and talk you out of your emotions. Why let people, who usually have their own esteem issues, tell you who you are and what you're worth? They didn't create you and they aren't in control of your life. God is! And when you are faced with low self-esteem, remind yourself of the promises God has given you. Talk your way out of the insecurities that say you can't do something or that you are ugly and worthless.

For me, I had to talk to myself and allow God to show me my value after something was said to me about my weight. It was during the year I was traveling with the Miss American Teen pageant. During this one event I had on a dress that a lady (someone I didn't know) told me I looked "big" in. In fact, she and another lady went on to tell my mother that I was too heavy to be a national winner. (These ladies had nothing to do with running the pageant.)

I specifically remember my when my mom and I talked about it. We were in the hotel room and I told my mom what had been said to me. She politely said that they had told her the same thing. Then she said, "What do you think about that?" I couldn't deny that I was hurt and a bit embarrassed, but I knew there had to be more to me than that. So I paused and asked the Lord for wisdom and strength to overcome how I felt. What happened next was amazing! I felt the Lord give me confidence and I said, "Mom, although it hurts that they would say those things, I am more than a physical person. God gave me this pageant title to give Him glory, and I don't want to fall into an image trap. I am doing my best to take care of my body, and even if they took away my title, at least I know I had confidence in the person God made me to be. This is who I am." It was the coolest feeling to know God had given me the ability to see myself that way. And it was helpful to talk about it. There are still moments of temptation to feel insecure, but I am reminded of how the Lord sees me and I remind myself of it. It's an inner battle that I can win, and you can too.

Lasting Thoughts

Being confident is a process. It's a process that you work on throughout any insecurity you face. If you compare yourself to others, you will never add up. There will always be someone else who seems to be better. You are beautiful because God handcrafts you. Take care of what He has given you. Try making this promise to yourself: "I promise to accept myself the way God created me. I will take care of my body by eating right, exercising, and maintaining a healthy mindset. Eating disorders are not the answers for my peers or for me. I will be an example of confidence from the inside out, with my strength coming from the Lord."

Speak Up _____

1. I think my body is in: ___ excellent ___ good ___ fair ___ poor condition.

2. I really need to: ___ be at my personal best ___ move my body ___ think before I eat ___ develop a healthy mind-set.

3. I (or someone I know) have an eating disorder. ___ Yes ___ No

4. I need, or I will help someone else, to seek help so that I (or they) can be healthy and confident. ___ Yes ___No

5. I will pray for myself and for others to have confidence in the beautiful people God has made us to be. ___ Yes ___No

6

Real Life Issues

Take what you learn from hard times and help others.

Dear Journal,
Life can be the pits. I can't believe I am going
through such a hard time. I have never felt so
down. Why does this have to happen to me? What
did I do to get into all this mess? I wish I knew how
to get out of this. I don't think anyone knows what
I'm going through.

—Lacey

*H*ave you ever had a really bad day? Not just a not-so-good day, but an I-never-want-to-go-through-that-again day? The type of day that makes you want to crawl in a hole and never crawl back out to life? I think everyone has experienced some form of a hard day, week, year, or maybe even a hard life. Some things you just can't control.

Think of It This Way

Sometimes life is compared to a book, a book that we make chapters in as we live our lives. Some chapters are better than others. I look back at many things in my life that I would love to live all over again. For example, I absolutely loved playing basketball for years, but now I don't play on a team. When I look back I remember how I felt after making a basket, winning a game, or just being a part of a team of girls. There are times when I wish I could do it all over again.

On the other hand, I also have chapters that I want to keep closed. Chapters that I know could have been better if I had made better choices. Like the time I skipped school to go study at the library. No, seriously, I did go study at the library. Little did I know that my mom would call the school and find out I wasn't there. Nobody could find me. They even had the police looking for me. Finally, the one friend I told where I was going confessed my whereabouts. You can imagine how much trouble I was in. My parents grounded me for two months and made plans to sell my car. (Thankfully, I got out of the car part. I just couldn't drive for weeks.) That was a bad chapter, not the worst, but a bad one. I look at those chapters and remind myself of what I can do to keep from ever creating another one like it.

Because every person is different, every person's "book" is different. Because people have different homes, schools, workplaces, and family members, not one single book will be alike. On the other hand, I do believe that there are pages that are very similar to those in other people's stories. Perhaps you and I have some similar chapters. Maybe you and your best friend have a lot of the same events in chapters. For instance, you may have both experienced the death of a loved one or a divorce between your parents. There might even be chapters in your life that you would never allow anyone to read, areas that are hard to deal with or that you are ashamed to admit to have lived. You might even be in the middle of a chapter right now. It could be a fun chapter such as enjoying junior high, or a difficult chapter like feeling lonely and depressed. In the same way, you could have just completed and closed a chapter; now it is time to start a new one.

What's Ahead

In this part of *A Girl's Life With God*, you are going to have the opportunity to look inside someone else's book. You can read chapters that have been written in the life of girls who perhaps are just like you. As you read, you may come across a story that resembles something you have faced in your life. The reason these young ladies have opened themselves up to you is to allow you to learn from their trials. Every story you read is true and genuine. These are testimonies of how God has brought them through a tough chapter in their book of life. In turn, these girls are giving God glory and helping others.

———

Divorce

When I was 9 years old my parents got divorced. I never thought that my life would end up that way. My family was supposed to be a family, not another statistic. After a while, though, I got used to it all. I was not used to not having a dad around at first, but then it seemed normal. I don't know exactly when, but over time I started to build up some bitterness in my heart.

I didn't even realize it until I was at a Bible study one night. We were told to close our eyes and think on things of God. The first thing I pictured was a heart and then I thought of love. Then I thought of the one person that I did not have love for—my dad. I just sat there for a long time and cried. I knew God could replace the spot that my dad left empty, but it was really hard to accept God as my earthly father. I wanted to talk about it, but I didn't know what to say or who to talk to. I just let things pile up on the inside. Sometimes I would pray, but something inside of me wanted to hang on to everything. I had built a wall around my heart and I wasn't about to let anyone take it down.

However, in the summer my youth group went on a mission trip. One night I heard a girl speak on letting go of things that hold you down in life. I realized that I needed to do exactly what she said—let go. I began to cry, and I allowed God to begin a work in my life. The rest of the message was about the chains that hold us down. It was all a wake-up call for me. The minister asked everyone to come forward, but I could not move because God was working in my life. God was tearing down the walls I had built and was filling me with peace and joy.

That night I felt so much freedom. I could not help but praise the Lord. There are times when those feelings of bitterness come back, but I turn from those past issues. God set me free. Whenever the enemy (Satan) tries to attack, I just remind myself of that night. More than that, I have God's promise in John 8:36 that says, "So if the Son [Jesus] sets you free, you will be free indeed."

—17 years old

Looking Back

Did you notice how this seventeen-year-old was not satisfied closing a chapter in her life until it was resolved? Her determination took prayer, time, and a willingness to let God take control. Now when she looks at her life she doesn't have to see the chapter of divorce as terrible and hopeless. She can view it as an obstacle that she overcame. The divorce was not something she had authority over, but the way she handled it was totally in her control. God set her free from bitterness and filled an empty spot in her life. He can do the same for you, no matter what the circumstances. Here's another person's story:

Self-Esteem and Sex

I had very little self-esteem during my teenage years, and I suffered from severe depression. I wanted so badly to feel accepted and important. When I looked in the mirror I hated what I saw. I was so depressed about my appearance and feelings of worthlessness that I was suicidal. I used to stand in the shower at night crying and banging my head against the wall.

When I was 19 my family moved. I was thrilled with the chance to start over. No one there would know what a fool I had made of myself. I met a guy named Johnny who all my friends thought was very cool. I knew that if I could get him to notice me I would find the acceptance that I had longed for all my life. We saw each other a few times, but most of the time he would call me when he was drunk and ask me to come sleep with him. I thought that was the only way I could get him to like me. What else did I have to offer? Our "relationship" only lasted five months. I never found popularity or acceptance through having sex with him; but I did receive something else from him.

Eleven months later I received a phone call that changed my life. I was told that I needed to come down to the local health department, but I didn't know why. When I arrived I was informed that a previous partner had tested positive for HIV. I knew it was Johnny and I knew what my results would be, too. Two weeks later I found out that I had also tested positive for HIV. I was devastated.

How could I face my parents, who had raised me in a Christian home with standards and morals? How could I face God? The news made my depression even worse. What was I supposed to do? Did I need to quit college? It seemed hopeless. My doctor told me that I would only live five to ten years. What was the point? I truly felt that my life was over.

At the same time this was happening, I was dating a man who was not a Christian. Even though he knew of the horrible disease and we both knew that we could never have children, he still married me. But marriage didn't take away my problems. It was after I got married that I hit rock bottom in my depression in 1997. My marriage was unstable; I wanted a baby so much. Worst of all, I felt that I did not deserve to go to church or to even pray because of the way I had treated God. I had spit in His face.

One night I was lying in the bathtub contemplating suicide. I knew my life was worthless and I couldn't stand the guilt any longer. It just so happened that my husband called home and I told him what I was thinking. He came straight home and told me that we were going to church the next day. Thank God for my husband's decision. The next day we got up and went. That was the day I gave my life back to Christ and He immediately delivered me from a ten-year depression. Glory to God!

God healed my marriage and has given me a beautiful son, and God has kept me from being sick. More importantly, He forgave me. Now I know that God forgives no matter what we do, if we just ask Him. Nobody deserves forgiveness, but He gives it freely.

—H. B.

Looking Back

This story is an amazing testimony of the grace of God. H. B. thought she was at the end of her life, but God had so much more planned for her. What would have happened if she had never turned to God? Where would she be today?

Is there an area that you are facing that is hard to accept? Like H. B., you may feel depressed and hopeless. There is a way back to life. Jesus is ready to forgive you and to come back into your life. There are also genuine Christian adults you can talk to. You can pray right where you arc or find a trusted adult to pray with you. The only way to find peace again is by asking for forgiveness and turning your back on the wrong things you have done. If you need additional counseling, talk with a family member and share with them that you have repented and would like help. The worst thing you could do is try to work through your feelings on your own. Just remember that once you turn everything over to God, you do not have to worry. He loves you and is in control.

⇒◆⇐

Death

Two years ago my oldest brother, Craig, was killed in a car accident. I never thought that something like this would happen to me. I came from a strong Christian family that did not seem to be affected by things like this. My main question was "Why?"

I didn't understand why God would let it happen to me. My brother was someone I looked up to and respected. Everybody loved to be around him. I felt so cheated. This was not the first time I had experienced a death; it was just the first time it had gotten my attention. I tried to be normal around my friends, but I didn't feel normal anymore. I felt like anytime that I talked with someone, his or her mind was on the accident. Most of my friends were at a loss for words at the funeral. Even months after, nothing seemed to be the same.

Some time passed and one of my friends asked me to go to church on a Sunday night. I always went to church before, but things had been too weird. I decided to go because anything would be better than staying home and hearing about Craig. God used that night to bring my friend and I back to how we were before. After the service, I was able to open up to her and we began holding each other accountable in our walk with God.

Everything did not get better overnight. Some things were even harder. It was especially difficult to be around my mom. For months she suffered from depression and she cried a lot. It made me wonder what God's motives were in taking my brother. Questions kept going around in my head, but God was using them for my benefit.

Months later, I started attending a new school and I met a great friend. Her cousin was in the car with Craig during the accident. God has really used her. Whenever she or I are having a bad day it is easy to relate to each other. We never try to say, "I'm sorry," because that doesn't change anything, but saying "I love you" or giving a hug really makes us feel like someone cares.

God has been so faithful to carry me and my family through this time. I have learned to be thankful for things in life. I don't take things for granted. Every day and every person is special. I treasure people and time more than ever before. Craig's death is the most difficult thing that has happened to me, but God is molding me. It is not always easy and it may not ever be, but without God I could not have made it this far.
—14 years old

Looking Back

Losing someone you love requires time and healing. This fourteen-year-old is a great example of how to move on with the help of God and friends. Don't face grief alone or by holding it inside. If you need to cry, then go ahead and cry. If you need to talk to someone, go and share you heart. More than anything, pray that God would help you to not become angry or bitter. Allow Him to show you the good in every situation. Just as this teen learned the value of life and people, let your loss teach you how to value what and who you have now. There may be unanswered questions, but God says in Romans 8:28, "And we know that in all things God works for the good of those who love Him, who have been called according to His purpose." He takes what we see as bad and turns it into something that challenges us to grow.

Suicide

All I ever thought about was suicide. I did not want to live and I could not see the point of living. I had so many things going wrong in my life. I was a victim of rape, molestation, and divorce. Just one of those things is bad, but I had faced all three. And on top of that, I had lost my virginity to my best friend's brother. My body was not important to me and neither was my soul. In fact, I was not even important to others. Nobody cared for me. I did not know how to get out of my problems.

But one day I was introduced to Jesus. Thank God for sending someone into my life who cared about me and cared about where my life was going. I decided to give Jesus a chance. The day I gave my heart to Him I cast all my burdens of shame, hurt, and emptiness on Him. Since that day, I have never been the same. He has saved me!

Now all I want to do is serve God. I know I am not perfect, but I do the very best I can to glorify the Lord in everything. He took away all my desires to die. He has shown me that I can move on and be successful in life. Jesus is the only answer that will ever help you.

—Teen Girl

Looking Back

This testimony shows how a teenage girl felt there was no purpose in living. After being abused, used, and neglected, there did not seem to be any hope. But the story didn't stop there! She found a new life in Jesus. No longer does she desire to take her life. She wants to serve God and make something of herself. If you, or someone you know, feel that your life is not worth living, talk and pray with someone for God to do a work. God is faithful and will show you the truth that life is precious when you live it according to His design.

Drugs, Alcohol, and Satanism

There was a time when I was close to God but I fell away when I moved to a new town. It was like I was living in two worlds. One world was for Jesus and the other was for me. First I started smoking, and then I started drinking and doing drugs. I was very addicted. All that led me into even worse stuff. In eighth grade I got involved in witchcraft and became a Satanist. My whole life had changed and I hated it.

One year my parents made me go to a Christian camp and I was angry that I had to go. What would I have in common with any of the other campers? I found out when I got there. I found out that I needed Jesus in my life just as everyone else does. At that camp I received Jesus back into my life. At first I still struggled with all the addictions, but He has helped me so much. I have been free from Satanism, alcohol, drugs, and cigarettes for over a year. God is so powerful if you let Him work in your life. God forgave me and gave me a fresh start in my life. If it weren't for God's grace, I would probably not be here today. I want everyone to know that God is good and He can start your life over with purpose and purity.

—16 years old

Looking Back

This sixteen-year-old seemed to have tried it all. But she did not say that Satan, alcohol, drugs, or cigarettes gave her a reason to live. Nothing gave her what she needed until she truly gave herself to God. She may have been tempted to go back to her old ways of living, but she was not on her own. God saw her through and will continue to help when she struggles. Now she is using her testimony and speaking into other teenage girls' lives. She has turned her hard time into an opportunity to help others prevent it from happening to them. Way to go!

Rape and Abortion

At the age of thirteen, I had an experience that changed my life forever. One night, my friend and I decided to get high and drunk. That had been a routine I had followed since I was eleven. After we had gotten trashed, we sneaked out and met a few of our guy friends at the park. There was one guy who was not wasted. He was my ex-boyfriend, so I trusted him. He led me to a place in the park that was totally dark and away from others. All I remember is that I was scared because he started talking about having sex, and I knew it was something I didn't want to do. I started walking away, but then he switched the subject and we talked about something else. The next thing I knew I woke up naked. I knew at that moment that my life would not be the same because he took something away from me I could never get back! After that day, my life changed even more. I went to the doctor a month later and found out I was pregnant. I didn't want to give my baby up for adoption or have an abortion, but other people felt differently. So I got an abortion.

After the abortion, I felt so low. I tried to commit suicide on many occasions. Then one week my mom got me to go to church to see the Power Team perform. From the moment I walked in the church, I knew there was some reason I was there. I met a girl who became my friend. She took me down to the altar and prayed with me the most powerful prayer I have ever prayed. Even though I won't forget the night that I was raped, I do forgive the guy who did it because it's the only way I can be more Christ-like.

Now I am fourteen and very active in my church, and I thank God for taking me through those hard times. If I had to do it all over again, I would probably do it the same way because I can be open about the awesome testimony that God has given me. It has given me the opportunities to help and encourage anyone who has had something like this happen. Don't look at your situation and ask "Why me?" or " I don't deserve this," because you have just received the best-worst thing that could happen to you, an active testimony!

—14 years old

Looking Back

This young girl has one of the greatest attitudes I have ever seen in a person. For all she has been through it would be easy to be anything but positive. But she beats the odds. It is evident that she has truly allowed God to work in her heart and heal her tragedy.

If you have been raped or had an abortion, you are not alone. Other girls like the one mentioned above have faced some of the same feelings and trials you have. Allow the situation to be what the teen called the "best-worst" thing that could happen to you. It doesn't have to control the rest of your life. God is ready to help you forgive someone that has hurt you or to help you forgive yourself.

———◆———

Family Life

Four years ago my brother started smoking pot. I was devastated. My brother was my hero. When he started smoking he hardly ever came home. The few times he did come home he fought with my parents. I would lie on my bed and cry, covering my ears because of the screaming. Because of his involvement in drugs, he received threats. I was scared that he would be shot or stabbed. Sometimes I even thought I might be hurt. I prayed day after day for his life. I knew that I could not do anything but ask God to help.

Instead of getting better, after graduation my brother became worse. He started smoking crack and then he got arrested. He was kept in jail for months. But now that I look back I see how this was the best thing that could have happened to him. While he was in jail, he rededicated his life to God. He knew he was messed up and he was not sure where to turn. I am so glad he turned to God! Now we can talk and we are building a friendship.

If I could tell everyone something, I would tell them how drugs mess up the person, using them and the person's family. It was hard to face all the trials my brother put me through. It was the most awful time and it hurt so badly. But now God is a priority in my brother's life and we are a family again. I am so glad I didn't give up.

—Teen Girl

Looking Back

This teen faced a hard family time, but she did the right thing. She prayed for her brother until she saw his life turn around. It was difficult to be in the middle of fighting and drugs, but she did not allow it to stop her prayers. Never stop praying for those you love. Prayer is often the only way to reach someone. Many people won't listen to loving family or friends when they are in trouble. When you pray, though, God speaks to them from the inside out. Keep it up, no matter how hard it is! God *is* listening.

What amazing testimonies of girls who used the bad to share the good! Those were some tough circumstances. Have you faced any of those issues? Maybe so, or maybe you have faced an issue that was not discussed. No matter what it is, you don't have to see your trial as horrible. Use what you have been through or what you are going through as a chance to glorify God's work. He is there with you and will see you through. He will give you chances to share and help others. Let them know how you handled it and that there is hope! This is definitely a way to be above average.

👄 Speak Up

The toughest trial I have ever faced is

I understand that God can use it for His glory.
___ Yes ___ No

I can overcome any trials with God's help. I can start by

If I needed special help with a problem, I would turn to

I will testify and help others ___ Yes ___ No

7

Dream Girl

Live with your dreams and not with your fears.

Dear Journal,
I wish I could ice skate like the competitors on TV. They are so beautiful and they make it look so easy! Even though I'm sixteen, maybe it is not too late to start taking lessons. That would be awesome! No matter how much it takes, I think I can do it. I'm going to call around and see how much it costs and when I could start. This is exciting!
—Michaela

Do you have any dreams? Most likely you do. There is a place inside every person that holds dreams. If you don't believe there is a place like that inside of you, check again. I bet there is. You just might have to dig through past failures, lack of confidence, or negative comments from people before you can find that place. _It is in there_, but you have to look for it.

So what's the big deal about this "place of dreams" in you? It's where your future is. It's where great things come from, great things you have never thought were possible or you were capable of achieving. It's where God uses your talents and blesses your abilities beyond what you could imagine. Your dreams are important.

A Cool Story

Have you looked around and seen individuals or groups doing amazing things on the mission field, in workplaces, in the home, in the sports world, in the church, and basically all over the place, and wondered what got them there? I can guarantee that the things those people have accomplished didn't happen by chance. Somebody had a dream and started living it.

It's like two teens I know from my youth group. God gave them the dream of having prayer every day before school. They called the time Soul Thirst. For their first meeting, five students showed up. Over the school year, more students started coming. Eventually there were 25 students coming out to pray from 7:00 A.M. to 7:30 A.M. Some students in other area schools heard about Soul Thirst and they wanted to start it at their schools. By the second year, at least 8 local schools had started a Soul Thirst. The teens had t-shirts made and started a website. The idea spread, and there was even a Soul Thirst started in Arizona and one in New York.

How did they do it? The students say they felt God gave them a dream to pray before school every day; they went and asked the school administration if they could and where they could meet; then they called their friends and told them about it. That's how it started. And it has grown. Now that's some cool dreaming!

The Fear Factor

Just as it is likely that you have dreams, it's likely that you have some fears about those dreams. Dreams are often pushed aside because people don't realize that their dreams could actually be fulfilled. It seems that unless people totally know that they are going to succeed, they don't even try. That's a bummer.

Pastor and author Dr. Robert Schuller thinks the same way about dreams. He asks the question, "What would you attempt to do if you knew you would not fail?" Wow. That's a cool question that may not be easy to answer. *What would you do if you knew you wouldn't fail?* Most people would probably try several things if they *knew* they would do well.

Because people are generally afraid of failing, they don't even try. They ask themselves questions like, "What if I'm not any good?" "How will I know what to do?" "What if I mess up and people laugh?" and so on. But author and speaker John Maxwell says we have three options when it comes to fear. He says in his book *The Success Journey*:

> When it comes to dealing with fear, you have three choices. First, you can try to avoid it altogether but that means staying away from every known or fear-producing person, place, thing, or situation. That's neither practical nor productive. . . . A second way to deal with fear is to hope that it will go away. But that's like hoping for a fairy godmother to rescue you.
>
> Fortunately, there is a third way to deal with fear, and that is to face it and overcome it. In the end, that's the only method that really works.

Which choice do you usually make? When it comes to your success, not facing your fears can cause you to become your own worst enemy. And you can bet that your fears won't go away by themselves. If you are going to do something, you have to face and overcome your fears.

Your own fears can keep you from achieving what you want most, more than anyone or anything else. Fears take the place of dreams. But as Maxwell stated, the only way to overcome fear is to face it. You don't have to allow fears or past defeats to keep you from moving on in life. It doesn't matter what other people have said about you, what your background is, or what you think will stand in your way. You really can achieve all your heart's desires if you believe in yourself and don't allow your fears to control you.

And more than anything, God is with you. His Word says in Psalm 34:4, "I sought the LORD, and he answered me; he delivered me from all my fears." He also says in Isaiah 41:10, "So do not fear, for I am with you; do not be dismayed, for I am your God. I will strengthen you and help you; I will uphold you with my righteous right hand." Those verses are saying that if you trust and seek God, He will take your fears and strengthen you. What more could you need?

Here's What Happened

I have a story about not allowing fears to take control over dreams. At the national pageant, I was waiting for my turn to compete in the talent competition. The system was set up so that all the girls who played the piano went right after each other. So there I sat in a royal blue formal, my hair up on my head, and my fingernails as short as I could groom them. As I waited my turn to play, I decided that I should say something to the girls beside me.

I turned to the girl on my left and I asked, "How long have you been playing the piano?" She turned and kindly replied, "Fourteen years." My heart stopped. *Wow*, I thought. *That is a long time.* She must have started at age two! Then I turned to my other side and asked the girl on my right, "And how long have you played the piano?" (I should have known not to ask again.) She said, "Ten years, and I just completed my personal forty-five minute recital at Carnegie Hall." Gulp. I tried to smile, but I wanted to run. *That's amazing*, I thought. *Your own recital at Carnegie Hall? Hmmm.* I prayed that the girls wouldn't ask me how long I had been playing. It would be too hard to say without getting a knot in my throat and running to my mother! The truth was that I had taken lessons for three years. Yep. Three years. Total. I had messed around on the piano since I was five, but actually learning and playing? Three years. Talk about fear! I was terrified to play.

I just knew I was about to humiliate myself on stage. *How could I be confident knowing whom I was up against?* That's when I had this thought: "Play with your dreams and not with your fears." Meaning, don't play with what you don't have, play with what you do have. I knew the Lord had brought me to nationals for a reason, and I couldn't let my fears stand in my way. So I played with my dreams. When I sat down at that piano I played with passion. I played with the passion I had from my dreams to play the piano well and to win the national talent competition. I forgot about the other girls and I gave all I had. Besides, the worst feeling I could have would have been if I had become intimidated and lost because I didn't do my best.

And the outcome was amazing. I was announced as a top-five talent finalist the next day. I had to play again. And I did the same thing. I gave it my all and prayed for God's blessing. Two days later I was crowned the National Talent winner—Miss American Teen Talent!

Was it because I was awesome and deserved it? Nope. The talents of the other girls were far more advanced than mine. I honestly don't know why I won. It was a miracle. I'm not sure what the judges heard that day, but I do know that my dream came true because I didn't let fear overtake me.

But What If . . .

So what happens when your dream doesn't turn out with a happy ending like the story I just told? It's okay. There are two things you can do.

#1. Reevaluate your dream. Think about what you are striving for, why you are striving for it, and what the end gain would be. This can be hard, though. You can't allow a time of reevaluating to give you a way out by giving up.

When I was younger, I had to reevaluate my dream of becoming a gymnast. Even though I thought I wanted to be one, when I evaluated the dream, it wasn't exactly what I truly wanted. I had some unrealistic expectations. For example, I had taken lessons and practiced very hard, but I couldn't even do a straight cartwheel by the time I was in fifth grade. Yet somehow I was determined to be in the Olympics by seventh grade! But I had to face the facts. Perhaps being an Olympic gymnast in two years wasn't exactly realistic or even what I wanted. When it came down to it, did I want to live in a gym 24/7 just to finally get a straight cartwheel? Not exactly.

So did I quit? No, I reevaluated my dream. I chose to take a different direction based on my heart's desire. I had given it my all for a couple of years and decided I wanted to take a different road. That's okay. What wouldn't have been okay is if I had not even tried gymnastics or I stopped because I wasn't any good, even though I wanted to still do it. There will be times you may need to redirect your dreams, not because of hard times but because your heart isn't in it anymore.

#2. Try again. If you have been striving toward a dream and you can't seem to succeed, you must keep trying. You may say that you tried to do something and it didn't work, so you have reason to quit. But think of this person:

In the year . . .

1831—Failed at business

1832—Ran for state legislator and lost

1833—Tried another business and it failed
1835—His fiancée died
1836—Had a nervous breakdown
1843—Ran for Congress and lost
1848—Tried again for Congress and lost
1854—Ran for Senate and lost
1856—Ran for Vice President and lost
1858—Ran for Senate and lost

This guy had it pretty rough! Can you imagine going through all of that? But that's not the end of his story. In 1860 this guy, Abraham Lincoln, ran for the US Presidency and won. Yep. He finally won. And it wasn't a local mayor position either! After all the things he tried and failed at, he didn't give up. That's what got him to the highest position as the 16th President of the United States. Don't give up!

Dream On

Okay. So you know dreams are important, and you know how to fight off fear, so now let's talk about how to see your dreams come true. Think about your dreams as you would think of the enormous task of building a house. When I look at my house, it seems almost impossible to know how to do all that was done to build it. When I moved in, I didn't know how it was built; it was just there. However, just because I did not see it does not mean that the hard work of planning, buying, and building did not go into it. Somebody had taken time to learn what to do and did it—little by little.

In the same way, your dreams can come true by taking the time to learn the building process. If you know how to break things down, you'll know where to start and what steps to take. The following outline is a practical guide that compares the project of building a house to the steps needed in accomplishing your dreams!

Step 1: Visualize Your Dream Home

This is a fun step! Visualize your dream home—imagine what the end product would be. Before someone builds, they think through want they want. Would they like a three-story brick home with a large modern-design kitchen and a beautiful garden outside? Or maybe a cabin in Colorado with a fireplace and a lake outside would be better. In the same way, you can find out what design (dream) is important to you. What do you see yourself working toward? You will never accomplish a dream if you don't allow yourself to picture it coming true.

You can think as big or small as you allow yourself. Do you want to be a straight-A student, make the soccer team, or play the violin? Picture yourself accomplishing those goals. Imagine seeing your name on the honor roll list and bringing a straight-A report card home. Imagine your team, friends, and family going crazy when you score a point and win the game! Visualize a standing ovation as you finish a solo on the violin. If you can see it, you're on the way to doing it! Right now, take a minute away from reading, close your eyes, and don't think of any boundaries—*just dream!*

Time Out

Okay. Did you take time to think and dream? If so, great! But before we move on, there is something that I have to ask. What role did God play as you were thinking about your dreams? Did you think about Him at all? Did you ask Him what direction He has for your life? If you didn't, it's okay. But let's talk about it for a minute.

Let's put God and your dreams in perspective. First of all, God made you. As you were in your mother's womb, God was laying out your talents, interests, and characteristics. When you were born, you were equipped with your own unique qualities. So first of all, God really, really,

really knows you. He knows you better than you know yourself! Understanding that, God knows how you will be fulfilled in life. He has a specific plan for you. He has a certain purpose and calling for you to fulfill. And if there is only one of you in the whole world, you are the only person who can fulfill God's plan for your life. Did you follow? Basically, if your plans don't match up with God's plans, you aren't going to be satisfied, and neither is God.

What if you don't know God's will for your life? Relax. He will reveal it to you. He may tell you through His Word, through your prayer time, or through a variety of other ways. The point is to know that no dream you could have will be blessed as much as the dream God gives you.

As you dream big and use your talents, don't get caught up in the pressures of the world and what others want you to do. Do what God calls you to do. If He wants you to be a doctor, go for it. If He wants you to be a speaker or preacher, do it. He may want you to join the ministry team at church and give of yourself there. He may want you to start a Bible study at school. God's dreams are big and made just for you. Fulfill the dreams He gives. If you do, you will be extremely content and God will be honored. Remember this verse as you choose your dreams: Proverbs 16:3: "Commit to the LORD whatever you do, and your plans will succeed."

Step 2: Design the Floor Plan

Okay, now that you know how you want your house to be (what your dreams are and where they are headed), it's time to draw up the floor plan. Designing the floor plan requires details. If you have ever looked at a floor plan drawing, you know that there are hundreds of specifics. There are lines for every hallway, room, closest, and doorway, and there are even tiny little markings for outlets and telephone wiring. Those details are written down so that the builders know exactly what to do and where to do it. It keeps a visual in front of them to refer to while they work.

You should do the same thing as you are working on your dreams. Write out the details of what you want to accomplish. Take the time to write out all the specifics. If you do, you will have a "floor plan" to refer to as you work toward your dreams.

A friend of mine once said, "I don't need to write my goals down, I have them in my head." It's fine to have them in your head, but writing them down will help you maintain a definite focus. Marcia Weider, a national motivational speaker and author on dreams, says, "The more you speak and write about your dream, the sooner you'll live it."

As builders plan out a house, they break every room down in order to know what is needed for a finished house. Writing your goals works the same way. You can break down your dreams into goals that act as the floor plan.

So let's practice by breaking down your dream house into rooms. We'll call them goal rooms. You can create as many goal rooms as you like. Over the years, I have divided my house into areas such as spiritual, physical, financial, personal, and other. Take the freedom to divide your rooms according to your lifestyle. Here are a few examples of my goals for the upcoming year:

Spiritual
Pray more using a prayer list
Memorize 10 chapters of the Bible
Fast once a week

Physical
Sleep 8 hours a night
Work out three to five times a week
Cut back on sugar

Financial
Give to the church building fund
Put more in savings
Don't spend frivolously

Personal
Have a good attitude
Listen more to people
Live more simply

Other
Learn to cook
Clean out closet
Write this book

These goal rooms in my "house" give me a direction to start seeing my goals come true. For example, I have a dream to touch the lives of other teenage girls. As a result, I wrote down the goal to write this book. Writing down a book idea gave me a specific way I can begin to accomplish my dream. It is no longer a vague idea. I do not just want to "touch lives"—I am focused on how I am accomplishing it. You can accomplish your dreams the same way.

Step 3: Build a Strong Foundation

I hope you had some fun in designing each goal room. This next step is where real work begins. It's time to start the construction. So bring in the bulldozers! Now that you know *what* you are building (Step #1) and the breakdown of *where* to build (Step #2), take the big step of starting to build (Step #3).

As in most buildings, you must lay the foundation first. Laying a foundation is the most important part of building a house. The foundation must be solid and able to hold a heavy load because everything is built on it. In the same way, the base that you need to build needs to be strong and able to carry a heavy load. What kind of load am I talking about? I'm talking about the load of problems, discouragements, and hard times you may face. In order to carry those trials, you need a base made of *focus*, *hard work*, and *persistence*. These three elements make a strong mix that will support your dreams no matter what may come your way.

Focus

One of the best things you can do as you work toward a dream is not lose *focus*. I can promise that there will be distractions. With some distractions, it will be obvious that you should avoid them; but other distractions may be a little more discreet. The discreet distractions are the ones you need to pay extra attention to. These are the distractions that may seem good or perhaps *are* good, but they aren't best for what you want to accomplish. Take, for example, the goal of being a worship leader in the youth group. If an opportunity comes up to join the drama team, which occasionally meets at the same time as the worship team does, the person should stick with the worship team. Is it that the drama team is bad or a horrible distraction? No way! It's just that being a worship leader is the true desire and dream—so focus on that.

Another way to focus is to keep reminding yourself of your goal. Before a piano recital, it was not unusual for my friends to see notes to myself in my room. I would often take bright poster board, cut it into smaller pieces, and then write focus messages like "Practice—you know you love it!" and "Think of how good you'll feel when you learn the song!"

No matter how you encourage yourself, just do something to keep your mind and heart on the right track. And have fun in the process!

Hard Work

Along with focus, you also need *hard work*. You've probably heard that before. But it's true. Your dreams are going to take hard work. The old saying goes, "Anything worth having is worth working for." It's even scriptural to be a hard worker. Proverbs 14:23 says, "All hard work brings a profit, but mere talk leads only to poverty." This verse is not only true for getting money for work but it is true for the "profit" of gaining your dreams. You can talk about what you want to do all day, but if you work hard you will accomplish it.

When I started playing basketball, I realized how much I enjoyed the game. It was challenging, but I wanted to be good. It took a lot of hard work. Because I wasn't the fastest or best shooter on the team, I would run sprints after practice when everyone else would leave. In the fifth grade I did ball-handling drills in the summer heat, working as hard as I could. Of course there were days when I was exhausted. But I felt good about doing more than what was expected. And it paid off in the years I continued to play basketball.

The times you choose to do more than what's expected or average are usually the times that no one knows about except you. It may be that you wake up early to review your notes before school, give up TV so you can practice, or stay back when your friends go out so you can work. Others may not know what you have given up, but you will, and everyone will know see the outcome of your work. Galatians 6:7b tells us, "A man reaps what he sows." What that means is that your hard work will not be in vain. If you work at something (as in sowing seed in the ground) you will benefit from it (as in reaping a harvest of food). What you put into it is what you will get out of it.

Persistence

Persistence is the final element in the foundation mix. Once you're focused and working hard, don't quit after a few days, weeks, or even months; you can make it. Sometimes it might feel as if you are reaching out to a vapor, but you aren't. When you're about to give up is when you should fight the hardest. Right before you feel you can't go on is when you should pull through. Remember these words from John Maxwell:

> The good news is that you don't have to be born with persistence to have it. It's an attitude you can develop and strengthen. If you're inclined to *give in* instead of *dig in*, increase your persistence level by doing some of the following: develop character, focus on the big picture, get rid of excuses, understand the odds, and stay hungry [for your dream].

People are going to say things that discourage you. Your family may not believe in you. You may not think you have what it takes. Others who have done what you want to do may intimidate you by their success. Whatever negative thoughts or words come your way—forget about them. Keep on trying. Keep on learning. Keep on keeping on.

Robin Jones Gunn is a great example of keeping on and persistence. Perhaps you have heard of her. Robin Jones Gunn is an author of teen fiction books.

I read how Robin Jones Gunn became an author in a book called *Behind the Stories* by Diane Eble. In that book I found that Robin faced times of doubt and discouragement. She worked for two years on her first book for teenage girls. When she was finally ready to have it published, she sent it off but was rejected. So she tried again. And again. And again. In fact, she tried several more times. And the book was rejected a total of ten times! "I was almost ready to give up," Robin admits. But she didn't. She stuck with her dream.

Because Robin didn't give up, she has written dozens of works that have been published. Her writings include the Christy Miller Series, the Sierra Jensen Series, and the Glenbrooke Series. She has also written over sixty articles, several gift books, and fourteen books for children. Wow. She is one busy and talented lady! But as you read, you see that she didn't do those things and become who she is overnight. Robin Jones Gunn kept on keeping on.

As You Build

If you have followed the steps above, your dreams are well on their way to being accomplished. Look for tools that can help you get started. Maybe to help get things going, you could read a book on a particular interest, talk to a trusted adult for advice, save money for lessons, or join a team or ministry that is doing what you want to be doing. Just as it takes more than one person to build a house, it will take more than you to build your dreams. You're going to need some help and perhaps some direction. Ask for encouragement from friends and family. Who knows, you could inspire them to start living with their dreams!

Above all, Jesus is there with you. He is your greatest helper. He is like the support beams that hold all the rooms together. He wants more than anything to see your dreams come true. Why? He placed those dreams in your heart. Psalm 37:4 says, "Delight yourself in the LORD and he will give you the desires of your heart." He knows what you want and He's waiting for you to ask and act. By delighting in Him and giving Him all the glory, you will see dreams come true. The fun part is reflecting back and checking off what you, by God's grace, have accomplished!

👄 Speak Up: _____

1. I took the time to search my heart and discover my dreams. ___ Yes ___ No

2. I wrote down my goals and will remember to look them over. ___ Yes ___ No

3. I will focus, work, and be persistent. ___ Yes ___ No

4. I need to remember to not let _____ keep me from my dreams.

5. In order to achieve my goals, I need to stop _____ _____ and start achieving my dreams by _____.

8

Visible Virtue

True success is living with 100% integrity every day.

Dear Journal,

Mom just had the ladies in her Bible study over again. When they first started coming I didn't like it. They meet in the den for hours! Not only can I not watch TV while they are here, but I can't get to the kitchen because it's on the other side of the den. No shows and no food—not a good combo. But I've been thinking lately. Maybe it's not so bad having the Bible study ladies at my house. I've actually started to enjoy hearing their prayers. They pray and talk about everything. But it seems that the ladies are so godly and are strong wives and mothers. Mom calls women like that "Proverbs 31 women." Maybe it wouldn't be such a bad idea to be like that. In fact, it seems to be a powerful way of living. I guess having the Bible study at my house hasn't been as bad as I once thought. Perhaps one day I will become a "Proverbs 31 woman."

—Missy

*H*ave you ever met anyone who had a walk with God that you respected? Perhaps it is someone in leadership at your church, a friend, or maybe someone you have read about. Most likely, you have been exposed to someone who has been an example of a godly person.

For Me

Last year I attended a women's conference for ladies in ministry. It was my first time to attend one, and it had a great impact on me. There were hundreds of women from all over the world. There were missionaries, pastors' wives, ministers, teachers, and evangelists—and all were women! I had a chance to hear from some of the most outstanding women of God. When I left that weekend I walked away with one thought. I thought, "I want to be a godly woman. With God's help, I want to do something worthwhile for the glory of God. If those women, who talked about their trials and difficulties, could make it, by God's grace, so can I." I felt motivated and empowered to be a godly young woman more than ever before.

For You

How about you? What do you want for your life? Do you want to go through life leisurely or do you want to grow up to be a virtuous woman filled with God's power? My prayer is that you desire to be virtuous. It is available to any girl who is willing to let God work in her.

You are probably also aware of the term that the journal entry above referred to: "Proverbs 31 woman." This term describes a lady who has the same attributes as the woman described in the Bible in Proverbs chapter 31. Although she is not a "real" woman with a name or face, the Scriptures are explaining some attributes of a godly woman, wife, and mother. But before you skip the rest of this chapter because you are not technically a grown woman, nor are you a wife and mother, hold on so I can tell you how it applies to you.

Here's how we are going to read through the verses. Instead of reading the verses as a grown woman, wife, or mom, I am going to take them and apply them to you as a teenager. We are going to focus on the principles behind the words. That way, you can get a head start on becoming a virtuous woman. The principles can be challenging, but they will teach you the basic steps of becoming a godly young lady. So let's get started!

Break It Down!

Proverbs 31:10— *"A wife* [or teenage girl] *of noble character who can find? She is worth far more than rubies."* Two things stand out in this verse. First, girls with character are hard to find, and second, if you do happen to come across one, she is valuable! Think about it. If you walked down the halls of your local public school and randomly picked out ten girls, how many do you think would be girls with character? I'll let you do the math on that one. Girls with character (a.k.a. girls with morals) aren't the majority. And because one is so rare, when you do find one, she is worth a lot! In fact, a girl of purity does not have a price value. She is worth more than anything in the entire world.

Ruth

If you have read the Book of Ruth in the Bible, you know that Ruth was the type of woman we are talking about here. Ruth was a woman of character. She was a woman of virtue. You'll have to read the whole story to hear it all, but here's the bottom line. There was a guy named Boaz who thought Ruth was attractive, but he knew that he couldn't marry her based on looks alone. But over time he learned of her character. When it came time for the relationship to begin, Boaz said to Ruth, "All my fellow townsmen know that you are a woman of noble character" (Ruth 3:11). Wow. Can you imagine? And then God blessed them by allowing them to be married.

Nice story, huh? That would be the same as you liking a guy (like when you're in college) and he finds that you are attractive, too. But over the semester he learns about who you really are and how you act. Then he decides he wants to start a relationship with you because of your *character*, not because of your looks. And that's when he says to you, "All the guys and girls on campus know that you are a girl of virtue." Now that would be a compliment!

Here's What to Do

So how can you have this priceless quality? Follow God even when it isn't easy. A girl of character wants to do what is right no matter what it costs. And this character applies in the big and the little things. For example, let's say you are in a video store where there is a screen that plays preview movies. All of a sudden there is a love scene with things you know are not right to watch. A girl of character would turn her head (or perhaps leave as quickly as possible) and strive to not even glance in that direction. Not only would this be her action, but also she would do it without hesitation. This would be a girl with a heart after purity.

Or let's say that you are at a sleepover and your friends start to gossip and look through magazines with lots of articles about sex. Having character means that you would stand up for what is right or you would leave the room and let them ask you what's up. When you take that type of stand, you are showing that you are a rare and precious jewel, and you are choosing to set an example. Your friends or family may laugh at you, but you will respect yourself and be more respected after you take a stand.

And more than that, God will be proud of His rare and precious girl!

Proverbs 31:11–12— *"Her husband* [or friends and family] *has full confidence in her and lacks nothing of value. She brings him* [them] *good, not harm, all the days of her life."* This verse can be applied to you in the area of trust. It says that people can have confidence in a virtuous woman and that she brings them good. That means that she can be trusted. People know they can be confident in her.

Can people trust you? Do they know that you are true to your word? Do you do good to others? Do you carry out the responsibilities entrusted to you? It you can't answer yes to all of these questions, then it's time to think about why and how you can change.

People Know

If you are aware that you sometimes lie or deceive, don't be fooled into thinking other people don't know what you are doing. People generally will know if you are saying something to get attention or if it is the truth. They may or may not tell you they know, or they may not always know every lie, but God does and it breaks His heart. He doesn't want you to have that sin.

I know a girl who lies all the time. She frequently tells things about her family, her problems, her friends, and her walk with God that aren't true. It is obvious to everyone that she is not telling the truth. There may be one or two things that are true, but it is hard to know. That is very sad. If she only knew that anything she says, whether it is true or not, has no value. A person who is dishonest is typically disrespected and no one can trust them. However, often they do not even know it.

Watch Out

In the same way, there are people who can't be trusted because they only look out for themselves. These are people who do things only when they benefit. It's like the story of Delilah in the Bible. The Book of Judges tells us that she begged and begged Samson to tell her where he got his strength. She used his love for her to deceive him into telling her. She said to him, "How can you say, 'I love you,' when you won't confide in me?" (Judges 16:15) But the truth was that she didn't want to know his secret so she could feel his love. She wanted to know his secret because the Philistines, Samson's enemies, said they would pay her if she told them how they could capture him. She was only looking out for herself and did not bring Samson good.

Do you bring good to your friends and family? Or do you do things to benefit yourself? Check your heart and try to see the reason you do certain things. Trust is huge in relationships. People need to know that you have their best interest in mind and that you aren't out just to help yourself. When you do things for others with pure motives, you will be blessed with confidence and friendships. Who knows? Maybe the more your parents trust what you say and do, the more they will allow you to do. It's worth it!

Proverbs 31:13— *"She selects wool and flax and works with eager hands."* This Scripture has to do with being focused. There are many things that are calling for your attention. You have school, friends, family, church, hobbies, and most likely a long list of other things. A lot of the things that call for your attention you have to do. But there are others things that you don't *have* to do. You may feel like you *have* to do them, but you don't. These things aren't always bad, either. Sometimes good things can distract you. One of the best gifts you can give yourself is the gift of knowing what to do and when to do it.

When I decided to enter the Miss American Teen pageant, I had to let other things in my life go. I couldn't do everything with everybody. So I stopped playing basketball and went out with friends less often. I had to focus on what I really wanted to do. Without focusing, I would have never even entered the pageant.

I have a friend who is the queen of focus. She and I met in the first grade. Her name is Caranie, and I have always respected her ability to focus. There were times when we were growing up when she would stay so focused, and I was anything but focused. She would spend hours on her homework, even in elementary school. Her science fair projects looked like they came out of a science museum! She played the piano and the violin and worked very hard on those instruments. Even when I spent the night she would practice one hour on each instrument (while I ate snacks, watched TV, and knocked on her door every twenty minutes asking if she was finished!). The girl is incredible! Because she was focused, she was the winner of numerous academic and music awards, Valedictorian, and a member of the Virginia Junior Symphony.

How was she able to do all this? She found out what was most important to her and she stayed focused on it. You can do the same. Find what is most important. Make a list of things you enjoy or have to do numbered from the greatest to the least. Then see if there is anything that you need to let go so you can focus on the important things.

How does this relate to being virtuous? It has to do with how you spend your time and effort. There are many girls I know who say, "I can't come to church on Wednesday nights because I have to . . . ." Usually it comes down to a decision that the girl made that she would rather focus on whatever the activity is rather than on the importance of going to church.

What is your schedule like? Is there time to go to church? Is there enough time to pray and read the Bible?

If not, then something needs to go. Priorities are important, and God must be at the top! Keep Him first, then set your eyes on the finish line of your dreams and work with all your heart.

Proverbs 31:15— *"She gets up while it is still dark; she provides food for her family and portions for her servant girls."* Did you catch that? This woman got up before the sun to prepare a meal for her family and a plan for her servants! You and I can learn a lesson from this virtuous woman: *A girl who raises the standard is a girl who serves.*

For the Lord
In Matthew 26 there is a story about a woman coming to Jesus and anointing His head with perfume. People thought that the woman should have sold the perfume and given the money to the poor rather than use it to serve Jesus. But Jesus' response was, "Why are you bothering this woman? She has done a beautiful thing to me." Jesus was honored at the way the woman wanted to serve Him. In fact, He was so pleased with the woman that He said, "Wherever this gospel is preached throughout the world, what she has done will also be told, in memory of her." And here we are talking about it 2000 years later!

How does that apply to you today? Just as the woman mentioned above honored Jesus by serving Him, you can honor Jesus today by serving others. God is pleased with you when you serve people. It is as if you are doing it for Him.

When it comes to being a servant, it takes a selfless attitude. It often means you must put aside your own desires. But learn to serve wherever you are. You don't have to be on the side of the road picking up trash or scrubbing toilets at school (but if you want to, that's okay!). Serving is as easy as getting your dad a glass of water or offering to drive your sister to a dance lesson. Just remember it can be as fun as you make it!

Proverbs 31:20— *"She opens her arms to the poor and extends her hands to the needy."* Give! Give! Give! The greatest pleasure is to give to others. In our society it is easy to get caught up in what we can get rather than what we can give. Rarely do you hear a person talking about how they wish they could give more.

Teenagers are especially known for wanting to get, more than their desire to give. It's not a sin to want to get something, but it can go overboard fast if you let it. There are some girls who think that they are going to die if they don't buy the new outfit in the window at the mall. You've got to be careful.

A Great Example

People all around you are in need. Perhaps you do not have a lot of money—that's okay. Money is not what giving is all about. Think about the story of the widow with only a mite in Mark 12. The widow only had a couple of copper coins to give the Lord. The coins were worth less than a penny! But she gave them because it was all she had. Jesus thought that was awesome and He praised her publicly.

You don't have to give thousands of dollars to make a difference, just give what you have. In fact, it doesn't even have to be money. You can give encouragement or a smile for free! And giving your time and energy is more precious than anything money can buy. When you give of yourself, you are giving a lasting gift and memory for someone to hold on to. Be aware of the people in your life and in the community. Spend time with the kid next door. Go talk to people at the nursing home. The amazing benefit is that when you give you will be blessed in return. Who knows? You might even want to do it again! Now that's true virtue.

Proverbs 31:26— *"She speaks with wisdom, and faithful instruction is on her tongue."* Earlier in the book we discussed the power of words. It is mentioned here again because of the importance of choosing your words carefully. A virtuous girl does not throw words around like a paper airplane, not caring where it lands or who catches it. A virtuous girl uses wisdom in her words.

Virtuous Power Play

A great example of a woman who used her words wisely is found in the Bible story of Queen Esther. (Read the Book of Esther for yourself sometime. It's pretty cool.) So here goes. Esther had learned of a plan that was going to wipe out her own people—the Jews. She had to find a way to stop the plan, but there were certain rules that she would have to follow before she approached her husband, the king. So Esther fasted and sought wisdom. When it came time for her to speak to the king, he was pleased with her and asked her what she wanted. He said, "Queen Esther, what is your petition? It will be given you. What is your request? Even up to half the kingdom, it will be granted" (Esther 7:2). Now was her chance! She answered him, saying, "If I have found favor with you, O king, and if it pleases your majesty, grant me my life—this is my petition. And spare my people—this is my request" (Esther 7:3). Her words were timely and full of wisdom. She had thought about how her words, and her words alone, could save an entire nation of people. She used wisdom and God blessed her. The king granted her the wish.

Wow! That is some major virtuous power! And it all had to do with what she said.

Proverbs 31:27— *"She . . . does not eat the bread of idleness."* This Scripture has to do with not being lazy. Let me first say that rest is a good thing. God intends for you and me to have times to rest and to be refreshed. Are you the type of girl who goes non-stop 24/7? You are the type who needs more rest. But there are other girls who love to rest and do a lot of it. This is not good. Lazy people don't go anywhere in life. Proverbs 24:33–34 says, "A little sleep, a little slumber, a little folding of the hands to rest—and poverty will come on you like a bandit and scarcity like an armed man." Too much idleness and your life could go to waste.

Mom

A great example in my life of a person who does not believe in being lazy is my mother. She is an incredible hard worker. I have many memories of her getting up early to cook us our favorite breakfast and staying up late at night washing our favorite clothes. I remember one time in particular when she was up mopping after midnight! Her work ethic is tremendous, and it has paid off. Her life has been very successful. She has raised my brother and me, helped my dad with his work as a business owner, and pursued her interest as a singer and songwriter (she even has a CD!). Because of my mom's motivation, our family has been blessed.

You

How do you spend your time? Is your goal to get up out of bed only to get back in as soon as possible? Are there nights you skip doing homework so you can watch TV, or you don't do chores because you aren't in the mood? These could be warning signs.

If you are bored in life, think about what you may like to start doing. There are hundreds of options to choose from when it comes to you being involved. After school is the perfect time to join a team or a community group, practice a hobby, or go to a church event. Just do something that will keep you going and improving. As you use your time wisely, you will be investing in yourself a life of fulfillment.

Proverbs 31:30— *"Charm is deceptive, and beauty is fleeting; but a woman who fears the Lord is to be praised."* This is my favorite verse of all in Proverbs 31. It tells us where true value is found. There are millions of beautiful girls in the world. And you are one of them! But did you know that beauty only lasts for a season? Have you ever noticed how women who tan all their lives look wrinkled and rough when they are older? That is because the beauty of tanning lasted for only a season. That's how all beauty is. It comes and then goes. It's alright to be attractive and to care for yourself; but do not forget that there will be a day when you will not have the same *young* attractiveness that you have now.

Through the Years

This verse in Proverbs gives the real value of a girl. It is not found in how she looks. Rather, it is found in her love for God. I know an older lady who is a wonderful example of this true value. She lives two houses down from me, and I have enjoyed getting to know her. She is a great-grandmother in her eighties and she is beautiful. Sure, her looks have changed since she was in her teens, but her love for God is what has lasted. Her heart is so giving. She always has time to listen to me, and she helps anyone she comes across. She fears and loves God and is always talking about His faithfulness. And that is why she is to be praised. Besides, a godly girl, even in her eighties, is much more beautiful than an ungodly girl in her teens!

As a young lady, develop your inward attractiveness before your outward attractiveness. All the beauties in the world can't match up to the girl who loves God. If you love God, you will have value throughout your entire life and into eternity.

Well, that ends our Proverbs 31 journey. It isn't just for older ladies after all! It contains some neat verses that apply virtually to anyone. Give it your best shot. God will help you and you will be beyond your years in maturity and growth in the Lord. Go for it with all your heart! When you do, you will be a girl who represents Proverb 31:29, which says, "Many women [teens] do noble things, but you surpass them all." Go for it!

👄 Speak Up

1. My life lacks virtue in the area of

2. Verse _____ taught me

3. What matters most in life is

4. This chapter in A Girl's Life With God has shown me

5. Learning _____ will help me as I become older and perhaps become a wife and mother.

9

Leadership

It's your turn to lead in follow-the-leader.

Dear Journal,

This has been quite a week! On Tuesday I was elected captain of the volleyball team, and today my class voted me to represent the sophomores on homecoming court! I am soooo excited! In two weeks it will be time to elect new people on student council. I'm thinking about running for secretary. That would be way cool if that worked out. But more than all of that, I want to be a good example while I am in all these things. I feel like God is using me as a leader at school. If people are going to follow my leadership, I want to lead them in the right way.

—Lindsey

Did you know that you are a leader? Yes, you. Whether you like it or not, *you* are a leader. You may not be like Lindsey in the above journal entry, but you are leading other people in your life. So what exactly does that mean? Being a leader means that you're an *influencer*. Being an influencer means that you affect other people.

In his book *Developing the Leader Within You*, John Maxwell talks about the fact that no matter what your personality is, your life affects others: "Sociologists tell us that even the most introverted individual will influence ten thousand other people during his or her lifetime!" Wow. That is incredible! That means that even if you are the shyest and quietest person in the world, you will still have influence, or leadership, on thousands of people. And if you aren't a shy person, just think about how many people you are leading!

Negative Influence

Now that we have established that anyone and everyone reading this book is a leader, let's move on to how to develop that leadership. Just because you are an influencer, that doesn't mean that you are using your influence in a positive way. It could be that your leadership is a negative influence on the people in your life.

You never know what your actions do to other people. Sometimes things happen that are bad or sad because one person used their leadership in a negative way. It works like what is known as the "ripple effect." If you threw a small pebble into a large lake, it would affect the water many, many feet out. Once the pebble hits the water, a ripple starts across the surface of the water. Often the ripple goes out for as far as you can see—and all because of one little rock.

Leadership works that way, too. One little thing can have an effect that goes on for as far as you can see. Take for example this humorous scenario: let's say your dad's boss yells at your dad for no major reason. Meanwhile, you, your mom, and your brother are having a great afternoon at home. Then your dad comes home for dinner and he is in a bad mood because of his boss. Your mom happily places food before the family and your dad says, "Is this all we have?" Your mom is immediately crushed.

She tears up and is silent for the rest of dinner. Later on, you are excited to share with your mom about your B on the science test. But when you share the good news, she replies out of the hurt from your dad, "I thought you said you could get an A on this one." You immediately feel like a failure and go to your room, only to find that your brother is into your drawing pencils. You are outraged, so you scream at him to get out, which makes him cry. His feelings are hurt, so he goes and angrily kicks the dog. The dog is now upset, so he goes outside and bites the neighbor's kid. The neighbors are so upset that they sue your family for having a "vicious" pet, and your family loses thousands of dollars over the lawsuit! Because you lost the suit, your family has to move out of your house and into a rented cubicle in the local YMCA, and there you all sit all because your dad's boss used his leadership in a negative way!

You may be thinking that there's no way all that would happen. Even though that story *is* a little extreme (okay, way extreme), many things do happen that could have been avoided if leadership was used correctly. That's why your influence is so important.

Positive Influence

In the same way we just discussed how a negative influence affects people for bad, a *positive* influence can affect people for good. As you go through your day, you can choose to impact people in a fashion that is encouraging and uplifting!

Think about this example: Let's say there is a friend at school who hates English class. She never gets a good grade but never really tries to do better. That's where you come in with your positive leadership. You approach her and challenge her to get a B on the next test. You tell her that if she does, you will carry her books around for a whole day. The friend gets so excited that she studies for the next English exam. When the test comes back she sees that she made a B! She is so surprised at her ability to do well in the class that from then on she starts to study for all of the tests and even begins to do her homework. Her success is so encouraging to her that she starts to make better grades in all of her classes. This continues throughout her high school years, and on graduation day she is honored as the valedictorian! Because of being top in her class, she receives a scholarship for college in which she goes on to study law. After receiving two degrees and graduating college with honors, she starts her political career and is elected in the Senate. Because of her success while serving the Senate, she is advised to run for president. Not only does she accept the advice and run, she wins and becomes the first woman president of the United States! Not only that, but while she is in office, she solves world hunger and brings peace to all the nations! All because you used your leadership to encourage her in school! Whew!

Okay, okay. So this story got just a little out of hand. But maybe not too much. You never know how your leadership is affecting the people around you! You could influence someone who is going to go on to do great things for God. What a cool opportunity.

Part I: Spiritual Development

So far, we have discussed what leadership is, who is a leader, and two ways leadership can be carried out. Now let's talk about the spiritual side of leading. As you go through your teen years and use your influence to impact people for good, who you are in your walk with God will affect *everything* you do.

If you truly want to be used of God and make a difference for Him in leading, this section on your relationship with Him will teach you what can make or break your walk. Technically, you *can* go through life striving to lead without having a deep walk with God, but whatever you accomplish will not last. And whomever you reach will not be affected for the eternal things of God. So we're going to discuss the steps to take in developing your walk with God. Then in Part II of this chapter we will go through some leadership principles.

Let's begin by talking about having a life of **devotion to God**. If you keep your devotion to God first, you will be way ahead when it comes to leading people. Why? Because the people you are influencing will see, feel, know, and respect the depth you have in your Christian walk. Not only that, but God will honor you and give you more opportunities to lead people.

Think About This

So what is devotion to God? It's a full 100% commitment to Him. As in, He is the number one priority. Numero uno. Primero. Alpha. Letter "A" in your life. Absolutely the most important priority in your life. Yep, even more than a boyfriend, job, or hobby—all the time.

I know that is easy to say and harder to live. The world demands much of your attention. But as you are faced with things that draw your attention away from God, think about how the world has nothing to offer you that will last. Look at the value of things in the world, such as clothes, CDs, and magazines, compared to the value of knowing God. Wouldn't you rather be living for God than have every outfit in the mall or every new CD?

Everything in the world will perish, but your walk with God is eternal. They don't even compare! God's ways are invaluable! This does not mean that CDs and other things are necessarily wrong. They are only wrong if they go against God's Word or take His place in your life. That is why God says in 1 John 2:15, "Do not love the world or anything in the world. If anyone loves the world, the love of the Father is not in him." But if you love God and place

Him as number one, His love will be in you and the things of the world won't be as important to you.

Here's What Happened

At the Miss American Teen pageant, I had a choice of priorities. I could've put God on hold while I was extremely busy with competing or I could have kept Him the priority in the midst of competing. I knew what was the best choice, and after choosing to keep God first, it paid off.

The night before the final competition, I felt like I should go down to the convention room and pray. I know, I thought it was weird at first, too. But off I went (curlers in my hair and all!). I started praying about who would win the pageant title. Then I went over to the judges' seats and prayed over the judges. After that I went upstairs to the "holding tank" room where all the girls sit and wait for their cue. I went to every chair and prayed that each girl would come to a saving walk with God and that I would be used to influence each one.

That was one of the coolest experiences in my life. Nobody knew I was there. Nobody watched or even peeked in the doors. It was just the Lord and me.

Is there anything special about me because I did this? No way. It's just choosing the Lord over anything else. Everybody has that choice! You just have to make Him most important. For me, I honestly believe that if I had not followed through with making God number one by doing what He asked me to do, I would not have won. And if I had not won, I would not have had the numerous opportunities across the country to reach teenage girls for God's glory.

Here's How to Do It

Okay, so how can you keep God number one? It's simple. I didn't say it's always easy, but it is simple. I bet you already even know what I am going to say, too. These keys to success with God have been around for years. You probably even sang songs in children's church that said these things. There are only two things you need to do. And if you do them, you are well on your way.

#1 Spend time with God every day.

#2 Go to church.

Wow. Profound, aren't they? You probably don't think so. But guess what? These things take discipline.

Time with God

It's amazing to me how missing a day spending time with God can mess me up. It's like I am a different person. I get upset easily and I can't seem to think about anything but myself. It scares me when I realize I have started my day without help from God!

The same is true for you. The more time you spend with Him, the more you'll notice a difference, too. You will find that your day is better than it would have been if you hadn't spent time with Him. You will be spiritually prepared for whatever comes your way. Even if you are short on time, every minute you can spend with God is worth it. As you sacrifice your time, God will honor you and bless you with enough time to finish everything you need to. It is an amazing thing, but it's true. You make time for God and He will give you time in return!

Ways to spend time with God #1: I know it can be hard figuring out what to do when you spend time with God. Even if you have set time aside to spend with Him, it helps to know the next step. There are actually a few things you can do as you spend daily time with Him. The first option is to **worship Him**. God loves to be worshiped in many diverse ways. Music is probably the most common way to worship. Psalms 95:2 says, "Let us come before him with thanksgiving and extol him with music and song." If you play an instrument, then play to Him in praise and worship! Sing *a cappella* or put in a CD and sing along. Just worship in whatever way you feel you can give God the most praise.

Ways to spend time with God #2: Another way to spend time with God is by **reading His Word**. The Bible is full of answers, stories, and wisdom. You don't have to just flip open the Bible and just hope something pops out at you, either. There are hundreds of devotional books that can help you stay on a pattern of reading the Bible and also give you Scripture insights.

You might know about a movie from a long time ago called *The Never Ending Story*. It was a movie about a book that was "alive," and it interacted with whoever would read it. People loved the idea of a book that had a mind of its own. But the movie was a fairy tale. The book was not alive and couldn't possibly interact with readers. But did you know that there is one Book that is alive and not a fairy tale? Yep, it's true! God wrote the Bible and it is alive. It has applied to people throughout thousands of generations and it applies to you today. It is the most amazing handbook of life. It is the instruction manual on how to live.

Earlier we even discussed some of the verses that apply to things you may be dealing with in life. Can you believe that a book from over two thousand years ago talks about things like gossip and lust? Pretty cool. And there's even more stuff like that in His Word. Just keep on reading and applying.

Ways to spend time with God #3: Another thing you can do during your time with God besides worship and reading is **prayer**. Prayer is simply talking to God and listening for Him to talk to you. It doesn't have to be fancy or sound like anyone else but you. There have been times when my prayers sounded something like this: "Hey, God. Today stinks. It's raining outside, my best friend is mad at me, and I have a headache. Even though I don't feel like praying, I love You and I know You love me. I know You are the only one who can help me to think on the blessings instead of all that's wrong. Help me to please and serve You today."

God understands and answers these types of prayers. He already knows what you are thinking, so you may as well say it (and say it like you mean it!). He knows how you feel. You don't have to feel pressure to talk to Him. It is as easy as sharing your life with a best friend. Even though God knows everything, He wants you to talk to Him about your life. All of your hurts, needs, friends, family members, grades, sports, hobbies, and anything else that is important to you is important to Him. He is always there and will always listen to you. Prayer is your lifeline to the one who knows all!

Going to Church

Here's the church, here's the steeple, open it up . . . and you're one of the people! Yep, if you're going to be devoted to God and lead others, you gotta go to church. Like, you know, *actually go*. Not go to church via TV or the Internet, but physically going to a place of worship.

Believe it or not, church isn't just something to do on Sunday and Wednesday. It isn't even designed for social club needs. I bet you know girls who see it that way, though. You know, the ones who come to church just to see if their latest boy pick is there? Although church *is* a good place to find a future mate, now probably isn't the time for settling down! The whole church thing goes way deeper than boys and activities. Attending church is one of the best ways to act out devotion to God.

Why Should You Go?

Church is designed to be a place of learning, fellowship, and worship. As a Christian teen, you can go there to learn more about God and how to live according to His

Word. You can find clean fellowship with other people who believe as you do. And you can worship God through prayer and music. That is why church is so important. God created the church knowing that it would be a shelter and place where leadership could help guide you in your walk. However, remember that not just any church is okay. The church you attend should be based on the Word of God. It should have genuine pastors that you trust, and it should challenge you in your faith

Some teens I know think church is boring. But church actually can be as exciting as you want it to be. It doesn't have to be a chore to go. You can find a place where you enjoy what is happening.

Teen Church

An ideal place for you to be involved is the church youth group, that is, if one is available. You can learn a lot when the services and topics are based on what you are facing today. Youth groups are like smaller, cooler churches made for teenagers. And I'm not just saying they're cool because I am a youth pastor's wife. If I didn't like youth group so much, I would definitely have looked into how miserable I would be marrying a youth pastor. I truly love having a youth group and you will too (if you don't already).

Also, by being active in the youth group, you can learn about God while having a blast going on retreats, mission trips, or weekly ministry trips! If your church doesn't offer these things, see if there is anything you can do to help it expand. Maybe you could help start a youth group, a weekly prayer meeting, or help raise money for a retreat. No matter how big or small your church may be, there is a place for you to be involved. And it is one of the best places to continue to develop your leadership. Besides, there's nothing like being part of a youth group that is crazy about serving God and having fun at the same time!

When it comes to being a leader, your devotion to God will determine the depth of influence you have. Staying close to God and being a part of your local church are incredible ways to be devoted. When you lead by example in your walk with Christ, you are influencing people in the greatest possible way!

Part II: Leadership Characteristics

Once you have begun to develop yourself spiritually, you are ready to move on to some practical principles of leading. Although everyone has influence, you may want to go beyond the average leader. When it comes to leading the drama team, running for council, or starting a club, you can have what it takes to be successful in leading others. If that is your desire, read the following basic characteristics of a good leader.

Good leaders are goal-driven. Without having goals, either personally or with whatever team, group, or organization you are a part of, you don't have a direction. However, when you do have a direction you will find that you have a reason and purpose behind your leading.

Good leaders are optimistic. This is also a topic that we discussed earlier (Chapter Two), but it is essential in describing a good teen leader. When you are leading people, you are going to face problems. If you are determined to be optimistic, you won't see situations as problems but as opportunities. The problems become opportunities for growth.

Good leaders are disciplined. Just as an athlete spends time disciplining and training the body for ultimate performance, you too will have to be disciplined in order to lead well. People can only follow you as far as you have gone yourself. If that sounds overwhelming, remember that little successes add up to big successes.

Good leaders are accountable. Proverbs 27:17 says, "As iron sharpens iron, so one man sharpens another."

People need other people, especially when it comes to people who are leaders. You will benefit greatly if you have someone who is keeping you accountable in areas of your life. What does that mean? Being accountable to someone means that you are open and honest about yourself and your weaknesses, and you allow them to help you. Choose someone who is far along in her walk with God as well as trustworthy.

Good leaders are continual learners. One of the greatest things my dad has taught me is to never stop learning. He has always encouraged me to read, study, and learn from others as much as possible. Even though my dad has been successful in the business world and in his growth in the Lord for the past fifty years, he still loves to learn. Learning is a lifetime journey. And the more you know, the better you are at using your leadership in the best way possible.

When it comes to this leadership thing, God is with you. If you love Him and strive to lead people in a positive way, you are on the right road. As you affect thousands and thousands of people during your lifetime, do it with all you've got! Use your influence to change your world. You can do it!

 **Speak Up**

1. Most of the time I am a negative / positive influence. (Circle one.)

2. I could be a better leader by

3. The area I need to work on most in my walk with God is

4. One way I could be involved at church is

5. Out of the leader characteristics mentioned, the one I need to develop the most is

10

Potential

You are the only one who decides what happens to your potential.

When I was about five years old I had a favorite song called "I Am a Promise." To me, it was the greatest song ever written. Even today I think it has some pretty cool lyrics. Maybe you remember it. The words are "I am a promise. I am a possibility. I am a promise with a capital 'P.' I am a great big bundle of potentiality." I can recall hearing those words over and over as I would rewind my Care Bear tape player every night until I fell asleep to the song!

If I could wrap this book up into a song it would be "I Am a Promise." Or, "*You* Are a Promise." Why? Because you need to know in the depths of your heart that you are loaded with "potentiality!" That is what this book has been all about.

It's about you taking the average standards of average Christians and raising the mark. It's not just saying you follow Christ but *showing* you follow Christ. But everything this book represents means nothing if you don't take what you have read and use it. However, if you do decide to strive toward a high standard of living, you have the possibility and promise of changing your world.

It's Now or Never

When I was growing up, my parents used to instill in me the concept of life as a journey. My dad would say, "Casey, life is a journey filled with different seasons. Make the most of every step of the way. We're just passing through earth anyway. Heaven is our real home. Use your life for God's glory and have fun in the process." Then my mom would tell me every birthday, "Make the most of this new year. You only have one chance to be this age. You'll never be at this stage again!"

Honestly, I grew tired of hearing those words every year. I thought, "Here it comes. The 'enjoy your life as you know it' speech!" But as I have gotten older, I see where they were coming from. It's true—where you are in life right now is not where you will always be. Believe it or not, you will grow up and things will change. I know that is so hard to understand as a teen. I bet there are days you feel like you will never get out of school or be without a curfew! But there will actually be a day when you move out, start a career, and/or start your own family. Is that weird or what?

So, knowing that those things are going to happen, you've gotta make the most of your teen years while you can. There are things you can do now that you will never be able to do again. For instance, you can walk into your school and witness like crazy and most likely no one will stop you—you're a student there. But in a few years, when you are in your twenties and you want to witness at the local high school, you will probably be stopped before you can get in the front door! And one day you may not be able to hang out with friends every Friday because you carry the responsibilities of a wife and mother. Not that the future won't be awesome, but enjoy these years!

God has you where you are, in this time period of life, in the town you live in, for a specific reason. You aren't a teen back in the 1940s or in the Bible times. You are a teen now and there is a reason for that. God wants to use you to reach your peers and your generation. You can reach teens that adults could never reach. You can influence students in a way that is relevant and that other people wouldn't know how to do. You can even reach people in your own home before you start your own family. Maybe there is a mom or dad who will come to know Christ because of your lifestyle. You won't be around your siblings forever, either. Now is the time to reach them. It's all about making the most of where God has you for this time in your life. One day you won't be there anymore.

Let's Wrap It Up

Okay, okay. I know I'm starting to sound like my parents with all that was just said. But I guess that happens when they are right! So, knowing your teen years only last a little while, I hope you take what you have learned from this book and use it to be a leading example of a Christian teen. In fact, let's go over what we have covered. As you do enjoy these years and use them for God's glory, I pray that these principles will guide you.

Chapter One
In order to make a difference you must be different.
This is the heartbeat of this book—the challenge to live differently than the average teenager. There are many girls who are not making good and God-honoring choices. You can make a decision to live differently and change the standard.

Chapter Two
Optimistic attitude affects everything.
Whether it's at school, home, or out at the local store, how you respond to situations can make or break your testimony. It can ruin relationships and even ruin your own view of life.

Chapter Three

Never enter a relationship that doesn't help you serve God better.

Who needs the world's standard for dating?! If you follow the pattern of dating that most girls do, then you will be left with the pattern of hurt that most girls have. It's not just abstaining from sex, it's a lifestyle of pure choices.

Chapter Four

Treat people right: Relationships are the only things you can take to heaven.

People are priceless. Relationships are delicate and must be handled with care. You have to be a friend to make a friend, have wisdom in choosing your friends, and follow God's Word when confronting a friend. In order to keep your family in focus, you have to view them as people and love them.

Chapter Five

Take care of yourself, but learn to accept yourself as God made you.

The only way to have true self-esteem is from the inside out. We have been given a wonderful body created in the image of God. When faced with insecurity, you have to decide whether to listen to Satan or God.

Chapter Six

Take what you learn from hard times and help others.

Life can be tough. You will face trials, but God can use hard times to work amazing testimonies in girls' lives. When you face a difficulty, ask God what you can learn and how you can use it for His glory by helping others.

Chapter Seven

Live with your dreams and not with your fears.

Dream BIG! Overcome your fears, let God place some dreams in your heart, and go for them! Apply these house-building techniques to your dreams: visualize your dream home (decide what your dreams are), design the floor plan (break down your goals into categories), and build a strong foundation (focus, hard work, and persistence are the ingredients).

Chapter Eight
True success is living with 100% integrity every day.
Virtue is valuable! True beauty is found in a girl's character. If you want to be a girl of high standards and morals, just follow what Proverbs 31 teaches: be a trustworthy person, a hard worker, a focused individual, a servant, a giver, a girl who uses wisdom with words, and a girl who finds her beauty in her fear of the Lord.

Chapter Nine
It's your turn to lead in follow-the-leader.
Everyone is an influencer. If you desire to be a positive influence, it first must come from your walk with God. That is why worship, prayer, reading the Bible, and going to church are so important. As you lead your peers, remember these qualities: leaders are goal-driven, optimistic, disciplined, accountable, and continual learners.

Chapter Ten
You are the only one who decides what happens to your potential.
You are loaded with potential! God has a plan for every stage of your life, and you are the only one who can make the choices that lead you to His will for you.

You're Incredible!
Well, you've made it to the end! I respect your discipline and effort to go all the way in the topics we've discussed. You are already above average just for taking the time to read about improving your life with God.

I challenge you to apply what you have learned. Change things that need it and keep on going with what you are already doing right! As you do these things, you will not only be an outstanding teen but you will enter your adult years with wisdom beyond your years, wisdom that will guide you and keep you on the road of righteousness.

YOU CAN DO IT!